Stephanie Lovegrove is a barrister at 4-5 Gray's Inn Square specialising in Housing, Local Government and Property law. She has over 14 years' experience of acting for both landlords and tenants in housing-related disputes, including unlawful eviction claims. Stephanie is ranked in both Chambers and Partners and the Legal 500 where she has been described as "demonstrating prowess across all areas of landlord and tenant law", "absolutely excellent: clients and solicitors love her alike" and "very sharp, picking up the important issues quickly".

A Practical Guide to the Law of Unlawful Eviction and Harassment

2nd Edition

A Practical Guide to the Law of Unlawful Eviction and Harassment

2nd Edition

Stephanie Lovegrove
BA Hons (Oxon)
Barrister at Law, 4-5 Gray's Inn Square (London),
Housing, Local Government, Property

Law Brief Publishing

Published 2020 by Law Brief Publishing, an imprint of Law Brief Publishing Ltd
30 The Parks
Minehead
Somerset
TA24 8BT

www.lawbriefpublishing.com

Paperback: 978-1-913715-23-6

For Alexandra

PREFACE

The impact of unlawful eviction can be devastating both for individuals and families and, for this reason, it is incredibly important that lawyers have a clear understanding of how the law and procedure in this area works so that timeous and realistic advice can be given and urgent steps taken (where appropriate) to safeguard a person's home and personal possessions.

Whilst there are exceptional specialist firms of solicitors (and law centres) out there which deal with unlawful eviction claims day-in, day-out, the difficulty many victims of unlawful eviction face is that such advice is no longer local to them. Once evicted, a person's instinct will be to approach local law firms for assistance. One of the aims of this book is to provide the lawyers who work in those firms and law centres with the tools needed to give advice quickly and manage claims effectively.

Thanks go to Tim Kevan for letting me do this again and to Garry Wright for understanding that writing a book and home-schooling a seven-year-old are mutually exclusive endeavours.

I also give thanks to my family: my parents and step-parents for their unwavering support and generosity; my brother for his kindness; and my daughter for reminding me that Nerf wars are way more fun than writing.

Finally, I continue to be in awe of the commitment and ability shown by my colleagues in chambers. I am especially grateful to Tim Straker QC, Satinder Hunjan QC, Vicky Thompson and everyone in the clerking and administration team, all of whom continue to take 4-5 Gray's Inn Square from strength to strength.

The law is accurate as at 10 June 2020.

Stephanie Lovegrove
June 2020

CONTENTS

CHAPTER ONE
INTRODUCTION

The second edition of this book has come at a time when the risk of unlawful eviction is so real: the United Kingdom is emerging from a nationwide lockdown, having been implemented on 23.3.20, in response to a global pandemic of Covid-19, and only gradually easing at the time of writing in mid-June.

As a result of that lockdown and other measures, the entire economy has been adversely affected. Vast numbers of employees have been "furloughed" (placed on a temporary leave of absence) on 80% of their salaries up to a cap of £2,500; many self-employed individuals have been unable to make a living (with loans and grants made available to support them similarly to the employed). The total cost to the taxpayer of these measures is estimated to be in the region of £100bn. Yet, because the cost of accommodation in the private rented sector is around 41-46% of the average income,[1] most are struggling to meet that cost in full or at all. The housing element of universal credit is available to those who qualify after means-testing (having depleted any savings to a level less than the threshold of £16,000) but that is paid in arrears and many battle to secure advance or hardship payments.

At the same time, those sharing accommodation with lodgers or tenants are less willing to continue to do so given the risk of transmissibility of SARS-Cov-2 (the coronavirus which causes Covid-19).

1 When only household reference person and partner income is used (irrespective of whether there are other adults in the household), those buying their home with a mortgage spent, on average, 19% of their income on mortgage payments, whereas rent payments were 31% of income for social renters and 41% of household income for private renters including Housing Benefit. Excluding Housing Benefit, the average proportion of income spent on rent was 41% for social renters and 46% for private renters: Source, ONS UK private rented sector: 2018.

Whilst homeowners have been provided with mortgage holidays, there is no such protection for tenants and licensees. The Coronavirus Act 2020 extended the notice period required before applying to court for a possession order to three months: s.81 and Sch.29. Meanwhile possession claims have been automatically stayed under CPR PD 51ZA initially for 90 days (extended on 5.6.20 until at least 23.8.20). The build-up of cases within the court system as a result of the stay will result in considerable delays processing them once it is lifted. This "lag" will keep landlords out of possession, during which time they may receive little or no rental income, after the already five-month long stay.

Given the grave financial situation many find themselves facing; the fact that mortgage holidays will not last forever; the significant risk that thousands of people will lose their jobs in the aftermath of the lockdown; and that those in the least secure housing tenures are most likely to see that risk realised, it is almost certain that the rate of unlawful evictions will increase in the coming months.

In many respects, identifying an unlawful eviction is only possible if one knows what a *lawful* eviction involves. In very broad terms, occupants of residential accommodation in England and Wales enjoy contractual and statutory protections of that occupation depending on its type and the time when it began. These protections are known as "security of tenure". The legal position relating to security of tenure is an incredibly wide-ranging and complex area of law and one which is beyond the scope of this book. Practitioners are invited to refer to the Encyclopedia of Housing Law and Practice, Arden and Partington's Housing Law or (for a more readily accessible breakdown) the Manual of Housing Law (2017), Andrew Arden QC and Andrew Dymond.

By way of brief example, tenants and licensees of local authorities who occupy accommodation let as a separate dwelling as their only or principle home cannot be evicted save by the landlord complying with statutory requirements to obtain a possession order and thereafter the enforcement of that order by court appointed bailiffs: Housing Act 1985, Pt IV (secure tenancies) and Housing Act 1996, Pt V (introductory tenancies).

In the private rented sector, protection is now afforded mainly by the Housing Act 1988 (assured tenancies and assured shorthold tenancies) and, in some cases, the Rent Act 1977 (protected and statutory tenancies), both of which require a landlord to comply with certain statutory requirements to obtain a court order (involving a prescribed notice period) and if an order is obtained, thereafter to execute it through the court process.

Ordinarily, an eviction will only be permitted where there has been a breach of the tenancy terms such as rent arrears or anti-social behaviour or the property is required by the landlord and alternative accommodation is secured. The exception to this is found in s.21, Housing Act 1988 which provides for a "no-fault" right to recover possession against an assured shorthold tenant and, assuming a written tenancy agreement was provided and there are no circumstances barring the use of the procedure, to do so relatively quickly, after a two-month notice period, through an accelerated claim at comparatively low cost. For this reason and given an assured shorthold tenancy is the default tenure in the residential private sector, one is left to wonder why unlawful eviction is still as common as it is.

The minimum level of statutory protection afforded to residential occupiers of premises is arguably s.6, Criminal Law Act 1977 which prevents a person from using violence to secure entry to premises, however, in terms of *eviction*, the Protection from Eviction Act 1977 and/or the tort of trespass is the real "safety net" for occupants who have no (or limited) statutory protection of their right to occupy accommodation.

An eviction which takes place in contravention of either the terms of the contract governing a persons' right to occupy residential accommodation, or the statutory process to recover possession, will be an "unlawful eviction" for the purposes of this book. Likewise, the term "harassment" is confined to acts affecting residential occupation of accommodation. In many cases of unlawful eviction there are threats (of violence or to evict) and/or acts designed to compel a person to leave accommodation such as cutting off utilities, blocking off access routes, posting waste through letterboxes and so on. Such acts interfere with a person's ability to enjoy their home and are capable of causing considerable distress and ultimately illness to the victim.

The value of a person's home cannot be overstated: it is a place of sanctuary, privacy, comfort and enjoyment. People build ties to community from it and raise families in it. Any interference with a person's enjoyment of their home is therefore deeply distressing for them. With the "castle" metaphor in mind, the law has developed to protect the right of occupants in their homes, a key element of which has been the law prohibiting unlawful eviction and harassment associated with that occupation.

This book therefore provides a practical overview of the law and procedure governing unlawful eviction and associated harassment. Consideration is given to the various criminal offences and civil causes of action, remedies, funding arrangements, the conduct of claims and obtaining and enforcing injunctions (to prevent eviction, for reinstatement to the property and for the recovery of belongings).

CHAPTER TWO
UNLAWFUL EVICTION (CONTRACTUAL CLAIMS)

This chapter looks in broad terms at contractual causes of action for unlawful eviction. When faced with an allegation of unlawful eviction, it is necessary to ensure that the facts of the client's case stack up against the various causes of action which may be available. It is common for claims based on breach of the covenant for quiet enjoyment to be wrongly brought in circumstances where there is no subsisting tenancy agreement, for example. This chapter sits alongside Chapter 3 concerning claims in tort. Consideration of both is necessary to formulate or respond to a claim for unlawful eviction. The key to maximizing your chances of success in any claim for unlawful eviction whilst avoiding adverse costs consequences is choosing your weapons wisely.

The civil causes of action available for unlawful eviction can be separated into two categories, namely contract and tort. This chapter deals with the former. A claim for breach of contract will turn on the express and implied terms of the agreement, whether written or oral. What follows below is a summary of the two main contractual causes of action that would ordinarily be applicable in a claim for unlawful eviction.

QUIET ENJOYMENT

Many tenancies and licences contain specific covenants or terms which deal with a tenant's or licensee's right to remain in occupation of the demised premises without being disturbed or evicted. In the context of tenancies, this is often referred to as an express or implied covenant for quiet enjoyment.

Technically, the right to quiet enjoyment does not apply to licences but each licence will be subject to its own contractual rights and obligations (whether express or implied) relating to interference with the right of occupation. The fact that a purported licence includes reference to the occupant being entitled to quiet enjoyment of the premises is a strong indicator that the occupant enjoys exclusive possession of the premises and therefore is a tenant: see e.g. *National Car Parks Ltd v Trinity Development Co (Banbury) Ltd* [2001] EWCA Civ 1686; [2002] 2 P. & C.R. 18.

What is meant by the phrase "quiet enjoyment"

In the absence of an express covenant for quiet enjoyment, a tenancy contains an implied covenant which, for the purposes of unlawful eviction or harassment, is in broadly the same terms.

In *Kenny v Preen* [1963] 1 QB 499, CA, Pearson LJ observed (at p.511):

> *"The implied covenant for quiet enjoyment is not an absolute covenant protecting a tenant against eviction or interference by anybody, but is a qualified covenant protecting the tenant against interference with the tenant's quiet and peaceful possession and enjoyment of the premises by the landlord or persons claiming, through or under the landlord. The basis of it is that the landlord, by letting the premises, confers on the tenant the right of possession during the term and impliedly promises not to interfere with the tenant's exercise and use of the right of possession during the term. I think the word "enjoy" used in this connection is a translation of the Latin word "fruor" and refers to the exercise and use of the right and having the full benefit of it, rather than to deriving pleasure from it.*
>
> *The nature of the implied covenant was explained in Budd-Scott v. Daniell [1902] 2 K.B. 351, 351-356; 18 T.L.R. 675, D.C. in judgments of a Divisional Court. Lord Alverstone C.J. said: "Apart from authority it would certainly seem, on principle and in common sense, that when one person agrees to give possession of his house for a time to another, that ought to carry with it an agreement that he, the*

> *landlord, and those claiming through him, will not dispossess the tenant during that time. Therefore, unless there is some special meaning attached to the word 'demise,' the good sense of the thing would seem to be that, upon an agreement to let, a covenant or contract was to be implied that the landlord and those claiming under him would not disturb the possession of the tenant. Unless driven to do so by authority, I should hesitate a long time before drawing any distinction in that respect between the words 'agree to let' and 'demise'."*

The covenant therefore operates as a promise by the landlord (or those claiming through or under him, but not a superior landlord) not to interfere with the tenant's exercise and use of the right of possession during the term.

Where, however, there is an express covenant, it *excludes* the implied covenant: *Line v Stephenson* (1838) 4 Bing NC 678; 5 Bing NC 183; *Miller v Emcer Products* [1956] Ch 304. For practical purposes this is unlikely to make a difference in a claim for unlawful eviction save, for example it may exclude a superior landlord's liability for those deriving title under him or it may confer liability on a superior landlord. The terms of the lease must be scrutinised carefully to ascertain who may be liable for acts interfering with the tenants' quiet enjoyment of the premises. An example of a lease inadvertently conferring liability on a superior landlord is found in *Queensway Marketing Ltd v Associated Restaurants Ltd* (1984) 271 E.G. 1106, (Ch) where the covenant for quiet enjoyment referred to the landlord but the lease defined "landlord" to include superior landlords.

Performance of tenant covenants not a condition precedent

The usual form of covenant for quiet enjoyment provides that the tenant is to have quiet enjoyment subject to the qualification of "the Tenant paying the rent hereby reserved and observing and performing the Tenant covenants." This does not make the payment of rent, etc., a condition precedent to the performance of the covenant by the landlord: *Hayes v Bickerstaff* (1669) Vaugh 118; *Edge v Boileau* (1885)

117; *Taylor v Webb* [1937] 2 KB 283 (reversed on appeal on a different point [1937] 2 KB 290). Resultantly, where tenants are unlawfully evicted on the pretext that they owe rent arrears, this has no effect on the validity of their claim in contract (though as we will see, it may make a difference to the amount of damages ultimately recovered).

It might be argued that this result is the product of the specific words used but it is apparent from the discussion in *Yorkbrook Investments Limited v Batten* [1986) 18 H.L.R. 25, CA (concerning the construction of service charge provisions) and citation of Foa's General Law of Landlord and Tenant, 8th Ed., that "the question whether liability in respect of one covenant in a lease is contingent or not upon the performance of another is to be decided, not upon technical words, nor upon the relative position of the covenants in the case, but upon the intentions of the parties to be gathered from the whole instrument." In the context of quiet enjoyment, it is axiomatic that a tenant's possession of the demise is not unlawfully disturbed. The construction of any such covenant must therefore take place in the light of the various statutory restrictions and remedies available to landlords to remedy non-payment of rent such as taking possession proceedings in reliance on one of the rent-related grounds or bringing a money claim.

This issue is all the more important in the current climate. At the time of writing,[1] residential possession claims (amongst others) have been stayed for 90 days owing to the Coronavirus/COVID-19 global pandemic and will remain stayed for another two at least until 23.8.20: CPR PD 51Z (implemented on 26.3.20); MHCLG Announcement of Robert Buckland QC MP, and Robert Jenrick MP on 5.6.20. Additionally, the Coronavirus Act 2020 prevents *inter alia* private sector landlords from serving notices to terminate residential tenancies of premises in England and Wales until at least 30.9.20. This restriction applies to the service of notices under ss.8 and 21, Housing Act 1988 and requires a landlord to give at least 3 months' notice in the prescribed form: s.81 and Sch.29, Coronavirus Act 2020.

1 June 2020.

It is a sad fact that some unscrupulous landlords, faced with tenants defaulting on their rent payments owing to their inability to generate income during the pandemic (as a result of illness, the closure of businesses and/or schools and lockdown restrictions) will not adhere to the law and will look to maximise their returns by evicting tenants in spite of the above provisions. The mere fact of such arrears accruing is *not* a justification for taking steps to unlawfully evict occupants.

Breach of the covenant

Unlawful eviction amounts to a breach of the covenant for quiet enjoyment. In many respects, it is the very thing the covenant is designed to prevent.

Acts falling short of unlawful eviction (whether they culminate in the tenant ceasing to occupy the premises or not) can also amount to a breach of the covenant albeit whether they do is a question of fact and degree. This issue is looked at in more detail in Chapter 5.

This is illustrated in *Kenny v Preen* (above) where Pearson LJ held (at pp. 512-513):

> *"I would decide on two grounds in favour of the tenant's contention that there was, in this case, a breach of the covenant for quiet enjoyment. First, there was a deliberate and persistent attempt by the landlord to drive the tenant out of her possession of the premises by persecution and intimidation, and intimidation included threats of physical eviction of the tenant and removal of her belongings. In my view that course of conduct by the landlord seriously interfered with the tenant's proper freedom of action in exercising her right of possession, and tended to deprive her of the full benefit of it, and was an invasion of her rights as tenant to remain in possession undisturbed, and so would in itself constitute a breach of covenant, even if there were no direct physical interference with the tenant's possession and enjoyment. No case of this kind has ever been considered by the courts before, and I do not think the dicta in the previous cases should be read as excluding a case of this kind where a landlord seeks, by a course of intimidation, to "annul his own deed," to contradict his*

> *own demise, by ousting the tenant from the possession which the landlord has conferred upon her.*
>
> *Secondly, if direct physical interference is a necessary element in the breach of covenant that element can be found in this case to a substantial extent, as I have already stated."*

Whilst the direct actions of the landlord or his agents would obviously fall within the scope of the covenant, a landlord *may* also be in breach having authorised acts by another tenant (of e.g. a block of flats) which are prohibited under the lease: *Duval v 11-13 Randolph Crescent Ltd* [2020] UKSC 18; [2020] 2 W.L.R. 1167 (which turned on the fact the landlord was required to enforce breaches of covenant on behalf and at the cost of the lessees and would deprive himself of that ability by granting the proposed licence). Whether and to what extent a landlord may be liable for the acts of others is a question of construing the terms of the lease: see e.g. *Queensway*, above.

The importance of considering the terms of the lease as a whole is demonstrated in several recent cases looking at the extent to which a reservation (such as a right of access or to do building works) impacts on the covenant for quiet enjoyment. When assessing whether a particular act is in breach of the covenant for quiet enjoyment, it is therefore necessary to have regard to any express or implied reservations or exceptions within the lease: see *Jafari v Tareem* [2019] EWHC 3119 (Ch); *Duval*, above; *Piechnik v Oxford CC* [2020] EWHC 960 (QB).

The decision of *Windsor-Clive, Earl of Plymouth v Rees* [2019] EWHC 1008 (Ch); [2020] 1 P. & C.R. 8, discussed below in the context of derogation from grant, is also relevant to whether a breach of the covenant for quiet enjoyment has occurred.

Duration of the covenant

When the landlord's interest ends, his implied contract for quiet enjoyment ends with it: *Baynes v Lloyd* [1895] 2 QB 610; *Schwartz v Locket* (1889) 61 LT 719.

Where a landlord enforced an order for possession made by a High Court judge in forfeiture proceedings by re-entry and the possession order was subsequently reversed, the covenant was held not to apply because so long as the order was in force it was to be obeyed and acts done under it were lawful: *Hillgate House v Expert Clothing & Sales* [1987] 1 EGLR 65.

NON-DEROGATION FROM GRANT

What is meant by the phrase "non-derogation from grant"?

The phrase "non-derogation from grant" is not confined to the landlord and tenant relationship but where used in that context, it means that a landlord cannot "take away with one hand what he has given with the other": *Harmer v Jumbil Nigeria Tin Areas Limited* (1921) 1 Ch 200 at 225 to 226; and *Molton Builders Ltd v City of Westminster* (1975) 30 P & CR 182 at 186; *Platt v London Underground* [2001] 2 EGLR 121 at p.4.

It is a covenant which most commonly operates where the landlord retains control over adjacent land such as common parts and acts or omits to act in relation to that land such that the demised premises becomes "unfit or substantially less fit than the purpose for which they were let": *Brown v Flower* (1911) 1Ch 219 at 225, as per Parker J; *Platt* (above).

Key principles

The key principles governing derogation from grant were summarised in *Platt* (above) at pp.4-5.

- There is a very substantial degree of overlap, between the obligation not to derogate from grant, the covenant for quiet enjoyment, and a normal implied term in a contract (see e.g. *Southwark Borough Council v Mills* (1999) 4 AER 449 at 467F where Lord Millett explained that the former two amount to much the same thing).

- One should give effect to "the obvious intention of the parties, so as to give the transaction between them a minimum of efficacy and value which upon any view of the case it must have been their common intention that it should have": Bowen L.J. in *Myers v Catteson* (1889) 42 Ch D 470 at 481.

- The extent of the obligation not to derogate turns on what obligations, if any, on the part of the grantor can fairly be regarded as necessarily implicit, having regard to the particular purpose of the transaction when considered in the light of the circumstances subsisting at the time the transaction was entered into": Sir Donald Nicholls V.C. in *Johnson & Son Ltd v Holland* (1988) 1 EGLR 264 and 268A.

- The express terms of the lease are relevant to determining the extent of the obligation not to derogate, and should, if possible, be construed so as to be consistent with what Hart J. called "the irreducible minimum" implicit in the grant itself. However, a covenant relied on by the landlord "if construed as ousting the doctrine in its entirety is repugnant … and should itself be rejected in its entirety": see *Petra Investments Ltd. v Jeffrey Rogers plc* (2000) LTR 451 at 471.

- What is also relevant are the surrounding circumstances at the date of the grant as known to the parties: *Chartered Trust plc v Davies* (1997) 2 EGLR 83 at 87C, per Henry L.J.

<u>The overlap between breach of quiet enjoyment and derogation from grant</u>

It is common for practitioners dealing with unlawful eviction claims to elide quiet enjoyment and derogation from grant because commonly, the two causes of action provide the same relief in respect of the same complaints (*Southwark LBC v Mills*, above). In *Windsor-Clive, Earl of Plymouth v Rees* [2019] EWHC 1008 (Ch); [2020] 1 P. & C.R. 8, we are reminded that the mere fact a lease refers to a right of entry enabling a landlord to enter premises "*at all reasonable times for all reasonable purposes*" does not give carte blanche to enter for any purpose the landlord might categorise as "reasonable". Insofar as such a reservation were relied upon by a landlord to justify acts which would otherwise amount to breach of quiet enjoyment or derogation from grant, the reasoning of *Windsor* is illuminating.

When construing an exception or reservation in a lease (such as a right of access onto demised land):

- that exception or reservation must be construed so as to preserve its validity yet as restrictively as is required to avoid a derogation from grant or a conflict with the covenant for quiet enjoyment;
- the application of the standard principles of construction will tend to lead the court to expect that substantial qualifications of the rights to exclusive possession and quiet enjoyment of the demised premises will appear clearly from the lease;
- apparently broad and unqualified words in reservations may, on closer examination, be found to have a more restricted meaning when read in their immediate or wider textual context
- if it is not possible to construe an exception or reservation in a manner consistent with the 'the irreducible minimum' implicit in the grant itself, it will be struck down as being repugnant to the lease;
- the *contra proferentem* rule operates only if the exception or reservation is ambiguous, in the sense that the court is unable to decide on its meaning by the use of the materials usually available for interpretation;
- if forced to have recourse to the *contra proferentem* rule, the correct position is that the reservation operates as a re-grant by the tenant and therefore the reservation falls to be construed against the tenant, who is considered to be the *proferens*.

The lesson to take from the above is that the extent of the covenant for quiet enjoyment/the scope of the grant is *not* determined by taking the express exceptions or reservations at face value but rather by first construing the extent of the exception or reservation in a way which does not go beyond the "irreducible minimum" implicit in the grant. In the example of a broad "reasonableness" reservation such as the above, *Windsor* held that "reasonableness" related to the relationship of landlord and tenant and so would be constrained by matters such as a right of inspection or to effect works of repair. It did not extend to damaging the land, cordoning off parts of the land, drilling boreholes or erecting structures on the demised land. Insofar as a landlord sought to justify excessive interference with the tenant's occupation of the premises by reference to an exception or reservation (such as refusing to admit the tenant whilst repair works were carried out), those advising either party should be quick to assess (looking at the express and implied terms of the tenancy) whether such justification was sustainable in the light of the above.

Breach of the covenant not to derogate from grant

In the context of a claim for unlawful eviction, the circumstances which give rise to the breach of quiet enjoyment, i.e. the landlord's unreasonable interference with the tenant's right to possession are likely to found a claim for derogation from grant at the same time.

It is also apparent from the above that where a licence to occupy is granted for the purpose of providing accommodation and nothing else, it is likely to be an implied term of the licence that the licensee is entitled to enjoy his rights under the licence without interference which would undermine the "minimum efficacy and value which upon any view of the case it must have been their common intention that it should have". Thus, though not expressed in terms of derogation from grant, acts or omissions which contravene the terms of the licence, express or implied, will serve a similar purpose.

The act of a landlord in entering premises without permission, removing a tenant's belongings, changing the locks and refusing to permit access are hallmarks of derogation from grant. Other acts, such as sending harassing text messages may more properly constitute a breach of the covenant for quiet enjoyment but not amount to a derogation from grant. Whether they will do so is a question of fact and degree. Depending on the facts of the case, it is wise in every case to consider pleading the two causes of action in the alternative for this reason.

POINTS TO NOTE

- **A claim for breach of contract will turn on the express and implied terms of the agreement, whether written or oral. It is imperative to obtain a copy of the most recent written tenancy agreement and ensure that comprehensive instructions are taken on what matters relating to the tenancy were agreed orally.**

- **If a client occupies pursuant to an excluded tenancy (or licence) then practitioners should look to the terms of the occupancy agreement (express and implied) to check that contractual and (in any event) reasonable notice has been given. Any failure to provide notice in accordance with agreed terms would give rise to a claim for breach of contract.**

- **The implied covenant for quiet enjoyment does not apply to licences but that does not prevent a licence from containing express (or implied) terms relating to the occupant's enjoyment of the premises (such as access at reasonable times of day to provide any services).**

- **The implied covenant for quiet enjoyment is a promise by the landlord (or those claiming through or under him, but not a superior landlord) not to interfere with the tenant's exercise and use of the right of possession during the term.**

- An express covenant for quiet enjoyment excludes the implied covenant and its terms dictate the nature and extent of the right; so, it might exclude those claiming through or under the landlord or include superior landlords in its scope.
- Performance of the tenant covenants is not a condition precedent to the covenant for quiet enjoyment. It is a breach of covenant to evict without due process a tenant who has failed to pay rent.
- The covenant for quiet enjoyment remains for so long as the landlord's interest subsists.
- There is significant overlap between the covenant for quiet enjoyment and the principle of non-derogation from grant. In the context of unlawful eviction (rather than acts falling short thereof), in most cases the two are virtually indistinguishable however practitioners should be alive to the fact that whether the act of physically removing a tenant from the premises (or acting in such a manner that this is the result) might fall within the scope of an exception or reservation.

CHAPTER THREE
UNLAWFUL EVICTION (CLAIMS IN TORT)

In addition to any claim in contract which exists, practitioners should always consider pleading a claim in tort. In a claim for unlawful eviction there are considerable benefits to relying on a cause of action in tort, namely, (i) the different approach to causation and (ii) the availability of general damages for distress and inconvenience, as well as aggravated and exemplary damages where *inter alia* trespass to land is relied on (considered in Chapter 6).

The following are the principle causes of action in tort which must be considered (and where applicable and appropriate, pleaded) in a claim for unlawful eviction. A claim in tort for unlawful eviction might, depending on its facts, comprise several causes of action the most obvious of which will include either breach of the PEA 1977, s.3 or breach of the HA 1988, s.27, but also trespass to land and/or the person, nuisance and wrongful interference with goods.

Protection from Eviction Act 1977, s.2

By s.2, PEA 1977, where any premises are let as a dwelling on a lease which is subject to a right of re-entry or forfeiture it shall not be lawful to enforce that right, while any person is lawfully residing in the premises or any part of them, otherwise than by proceedings in court.

This provision ensures that any person who occupies premises in a residential capacity pursuant to a lease containing a right of re-entry or forfeiture cannot be evicted by the landlord peaceably re-entering those premises.

It covers mixed-use premises where part of the premises is used for business purposes and part for residential occupation e.g. a pub, restaurant etc: *Patel v Pirabakaran* [2006] EWCA Civ 685; [2006] 1 WLR 3112; [2006] HLR 39, where the Court of Appeal held that the phrase "let as a dwelling" within s.2 of the PEA, 1977 meant "let wholly *or partly* as a dwelling" and so applied to premises which were let for mixed residential and business purposes.

In *Pirabakan* (above), the Court of Appeal proceeded on the basis that the section gave rise to a civil cause of action consistently with *Warder v Cooper* [1970] 1 All E.R. 1112. *Warder* held that s.3, PEA 1977 created an actionable tort (c.f. the obiter comments of Ormerod LJ in *McCall v Abelesz* [1976] Q.B. 585 CA and Patten LJ in *Smith v Khan* [2018] EWCA Civ 1137; [2018] H.L.R. 31 discussed below).

Protection from Eviction Act 1977, s.3 –

By s.3, PEA 1977,

> "*(1) Where any premises have been let as a dwelling under a tenancy which is neither a statutorily protected tenancy nor an excluded tenancy and—*
>
> > *(a) the tenancy (in this section referred to as the former tenancy) has come to an end, but*
> >
> > *(b) the occupier continues to reside in the premises or part of them,*
>
> *it shall not be lawful for the owner to enforce against the occupier, otherwise than by proceedings in the court, his right to recover possession of the premises.*"

This section provides that a landlord must take court proceedings to recover possession of any premises let as a dwelling where the tenancy has come to an end and the occupier continues to reside in them unless (i) the tenancy falls within a separate statutory scheme of protection or (ii) is excluded by s.3A.

Applies to licences

By s.3(2B), the protection afforded by this section extends also to any premises occupied as a dwelling under a licence, other than an excluded licence.

Civil cause of action?

Until recently, breach of this section was thought to give rise to a civil cause of action: *Warder* (above), considering s.32, Rent Act 1965 which is in virtually the same terms as s.3, PEA 1977 (see e.g. *Sumeghova v McMahon* [2002] EWCA Civ 1581; [2003] H.L.R. 26, concerning a civil claim under s.3, PEA 1977). This is in contrast to s.1 (discussed further in Chapter 3) which has been construed as only creating a criminal offence: *McCall v Abelesz* (above).

However, in *Smith v Khan* (above), seemingly absent argument on the point and without referring to *Warder* and those authorities based upon it, Patten LJ held that "[...] the 1977 Act does not create a statutory cause of action. It merely confirms that Mrs Smith's removal was unlawful." It therefore appears that *Smith* either proceeded upon the premise that s.3 was to be treated in the same way as s.1, PEA 1977 without considering *Warder* etc., or it shared the *obiter* views expressed by Ormerod LJ in *McCall v Abelesz* (above), where he stated (again without reference to *Warder*) that *neither* ss.31 and 32, 1965 Act (now ss.2 and 3, PEA 1977) "provide[d] a specific remedy for breach of its terms but the effect of them, as before, was to deprive the owner of his defence to an action for trespass" (at p.597).

The upshot of the above is that there is now a weight of *obiter* comment regarding whether ss.2 and 3, PEA 1977 Act create an actionable tort and the only decision where the point was squarely in issue and argued fully is that of the High Court in *Warder*. As it stands, therefore, advisors should be alive to the risk that bringing a claim under s.3 may be defended on grounds that no civil cause of action arises from it. The preferable route is likely to be to plead both it and trespass alongside any other claims in contract and/or tort.

The elements of the statutory prohibition are considered in more detail below.

"Let as a dwelling"

In order to decide whether accommodation has been let as a dwelling, it is necessary to consider the purpose of the letting: *Horford Investments Ltd v Lambert [1976] Ch. 39* CA. In this regard, the terms of the letting are the primary consideration: *Wolfe v Hogan [1949] 2 K.B. 194* , CA; and, *Horford.*

A room in a hotel is capable of being a "dwelling" within the meaning of s.1, Housing Act 1988: *Uratemp Ventures Ltd v Collins* [2001] UKHL 43, [2002] 1 AC 301. Lord Millett (prior to what is a joyously literary exposition) stated at [30]:

> *"The words "dwell" and "dwelling" are not terms of art with a specialised legal meaning. They are ordinary English words, even if they are perhaps no longer in common use. They mean the same as "inhabit" and "habitation" or more precisely "abide" and "abode", and refer to the place where one lives and makes one's home. They suggest a greater degree of settled occupation than "reside" and "residence", connoting the place where the occupier habitually sleeps and usually eats..."*

A useful illustration of the dividing line between accommodation which is a dwelling and accommodation which is not is provided in the context of local housing authority provision of temporary accommodation for the homeless pending inquiries into what, if any, duty is owed to them: s.188(1), s.184, HA 1996. In *Mohammed v Manek and Royal Borough of Kensington & Chelsea* (1995) 27 HLR 439, the Court of Appeal held that such accommodation could not, as a general rule, be accommodation "occupied as a dwelling" within s.3, PEA 1977; the general rule could be displaced by an agreement between the authority and the applicant, or possibly if the applicant's occupation was allowed to continue on *more than a transient basis.* This reasoning was upheld - despite the commencement of the Human Rights Act 1998 - in *Desnousse v Newham LBC* [2006] HLR 38, CA.

In *N v Lewisham LBC* [2015] AC 1259; [2015] HLR 6, all of the above was again considered by the Supreme Court in the light of the decision in *Manchester CC v Pinnock* [2010] UKSC 45; [2011] 2 AC 104, (where it was held that a court must, where asked, consider the proportionality of an eviction where the making of a possession order was mandatory) and the rule in *Manek* was upheld.

N decided that the word "dwelling" did not have a precise, technical meaning and had to be interpreted having regard to its legal and factual context and the purpose of the statute in which it was used; "dwelling" bore the same meaning in the PEA 1977 as in the Rent Act legislation which preceded it and as a general rule "dwelling" suggested a more settled occupation than "residence" and could be equated with one's home; and, in order to ascertain whether premises were "occupied as a dwelling under a licence" within the meaning of s.3 of the PEA 1977 it was necessary to look at the purpose of the licence in each case and the purpose of the licence (i.e., a temporary expedient pending a decision on a homelessness application and an ability to transfer applicants to alternative accommodation at short notice).

In *Dacorum BC v Bucknall* [2017] EWHC 2049 (QB); [2017] H.L.R. 40, Popplewell J held that whilst the letting of accommodation may not initially constitute a dwelling if the purpose of the letting is to provide accommodation pending a decision whether an applicant is entitled to the full housing duty under s.193, Housing Act 1996 (as amended), upon a local authority finding such a duty is owed, the situation changed such that the same temporary accommodation let under the same terms and conditions of occupation becomes a dwelling such that s.3, PEA 1977 applies. This decision is consistent with the *obiter dicta* of Baroness Hale in *N* (at [165]) and is not inconsistent with the reasoning in either *Horford* or *Wolfe*.

So, be aware that whether or not s.3, PEA 1977 applies to an occupation arrangement is capable of change, depending on the legal and factual circumstances existing at the time notice to quit or vacate is served.

"Occupier"

By s.3(2), "the occupier", in relation to any premises, means any person lawfully residing in the premises or part of them at the termination of the former tenancy.

This would include licensees of the tenant such as family, friends and so on so long as they lawfully "resided" in the premises (if there were e.g. a prohibition on occupants other than the licensee, or the person were staying on a temporary basis, they would not be able to sue).

"Owner"

By s.8(3), "the owner" means the person who, as against the occupier, is entitled to possession of the premises. This would include a tenant or licensee's immediate landlord or licensor.

"Continues"

Section 3, PEA 1977 requires that an occupier continues to occupy the premises after the end of the tenancy. Query, whether, if a tenant served a notice to quit which ended her tenancy and moved out but retained a key, changed her mind (e.g. because a job elsewhere fell through) and moved back in, the landlord would be obliged to take court proceedings to evict her.

Even if this were the case, a landlord would be well advised to take possession proceedings in any event to avoid contravention of s.6, Criminal Law Act 1977 (prohibition on use of unreasonable force to recover possession) which is considered in Chapter 4.

Exclusion of "statutorily protected tenancy"

Section 3, PEA 1977 does not apply to "statutorily protected tenancies" which have their own statutory codes governing eviction. By s.8(1), a "statutorily protected tenancy" means:

- a Rent Act 1977 protected tenancy;

- a long lease under Part I of the Landlord and Tenant Act 1954;
- a protected occupancy or statutory tenancy as defined in the Rent (Agriculture) Act 1976;
- a business tenancy within Part II of the Landlord and Tenant Act 1954;
- a tenancy of an agricultural holding within the meaning of the Agricultural Holdings Act 1986;
- an assured tenancy or assured agricultural occupancy under Part I of the Housing Act 1988;
- a long residential tenancy at a low rent within Schedule 10 to the Local Government and Housing Act 1989;
- a farm business tenancy within the Agricultural Tenancies Act 1995.

It is important to note that whilst a mixed-use tenancy (business/residential) may be excluded from the protection of s.3, PEA 1977 by s.3A (see below), it attracts the protection of s.2, thus preventing a landlord from peaceably re-entering mixed-use premises.

The effect of the exclusion of statutorily protected tenancies is that s.3, PEA 1977 is not a cause of action for unlawful eviction in such cases for so long as that tenancy subsists. So, if a tenancy is secure or assured/assured shorthold, the correct cause of action for unlawful eviction is s.27, Housing Act 1988 (considered below). The main circumstances in which a proposed claimant would rely on s.3, PEA 1977 are where they are a licensee with no statutory protection and not excluded under s.3A, PEA 1977, or where a statutorily protected tenancy has been ended by the tenant but the tenant or any person who occupied the property lawfully at the end of the tenancy (e.g. a member of the tenant's family) remained in occupation.

Excluded tenancies

Section 3A, PEA 1977 was inserted by s.31, Housing Act 1988 and excludes tenancies or licences from the protection of s.3, PEA 1977 in certain specified circumstances.

Shared with landlord

A tenancy or licence is excluded if it provides that (i) the occupier shares any accommodation with the landlord or licensor; and (ii) immediately before the tenancy or licence was granted (and also at the time it comes to an end) the landlord or licensor occupied as his only or principal home premises of which the whole or part of the shared accommodation formed part.

For the purposes of the above, an occupier *shares* accommodation with another person if he has the use of it in common with that person (whether or not also in common with others) and if, in relation to any tenancy or licence, there is at any time more than one person who is the landlord or licensor, any reference in those subsections to the landlord or licensor is construed as a reference to any one of those persons: s.3A(4). Also, *"accommodation"* does not include any area used for storage nor a staircase, passage, corridor or other means of access; *"occupier"* means the tenant and licensee under the respective tenancy or licence in issue; *"purpose-built block of flats"* has the same meaning as in Part III of Schedule 1 to the Housing Act 1988.

This exclusion gives rise to several separate considerations:

- first, whether the tenancy or licence *provides* that the occupier shares any accommodation with the landlord or licensor (which involves scrutinising the terms of a written agreement or any orally agreed terms);
- secondly, whether the landlord occupied the premises as his only or principle home both immediately before the grant and when it came to an end; and

- thirdly, whether the whole or part of the shared accommodation formed part of the premises.

It is important when assessing whether a landlord is resident to note the use of the words "only or principle home". Whilst a detailed exposition of the meaning of this phrase and its historical development is beyond the scope of this book, it is sufficient to rely on the *dicta* of Lewison LJ in *Havering LBC v Dove* [2017] EWCA Civ 156; [2017] H.L.R. 19 (at [18]):

> *"The courts developed the principle that continuous physical presence in a dwelling was not necessary to maintain occupation as a residence. It thus became necessary to lay down some guidelines to differentiate between cases in which occupation as a residence had been maintained and those in which it had not. Many of these cases are discussed and summarised by Etherton LJ in* Islington LBC v Boyle *[2011] EWCA Civ 1450; [2012] P.T.S.R. 1093."*

Where a person has only one set of premises available to occupy, there is little room for dispute that the premises are that person's only home but, uncertainty abounds where a person has two sets of premises available for occupation and maintains a presence in both. In *Boyle*, Etherton LJ confirmed that it was possible to have ceased to occupy premises (sometimes for considerable periods) and even to live elsewhere, but nonetheless continue to occupy premises as a *principle* home. The key question is whether, despite being out of occupation, the person has an objectively manifested intention to return sufficient to rebut the presumption which arises from his having ceased to occupy the accommodation for a lengthy time. A similar approach is taken in cases where a person takes up occupation of two homes (e.g. staying half the week in one set of premises and half in another) albeit in such cases the intention would likely be to resort to a "previous pattern of existence" (i.e. to return to occupy one property principally over the other): *Dove*, (at [22]).

In *Sumeghova v McMahon* [2002] EWCA Civ 1581; [2003] H.L.R. 26, which concerned a "two homes" case and the meaning of the exclusion from s.3, PEA 1977 under s.3A(2) of the same, the Court of Appeal held that where a person sleeps is of the utmost importance.

What is apparent from the above is that the mere fact that a landlord is not physically present at accommodation from which he evicts a tenant or licensee, does not guarantee that the accommodation is not "shared" with the landlord within the meaning of s.3A(2), PEA 1977. Advisors must be astute to ascertain the precise living arrangements at the premises as known to a landlord or an occupier when assessing whether this exclusion may apply.

Shared with member of landlord's family

A tenancy or licence is excluded if it provides that (i) the occupier shares any accommodation with a member of the family of the landlord or licensor; (ii) immediately before the tenancy or licence was granted and also at the time it comes to an end, the member of the family of the landlord or licensor occupied as his only or principal home premises of which the whole or part of the shared accommodation formed part; and (ii) immediately before the tenancy or licence was granted and also at the time it comes to an end, the landlord or licensor occupied as his only or principal home premises in the same building as the shared accommodation and that building is not a purpose-built block of flats.

The definitions of "shared", "accommodation", "occupier" and "purpose-built block of flats" referred to above apply here.

Consistently with s.113, HA 1985, *"family member"* means a spouse, civil partner, cohabitant, parent, grandparent, child, grandchild, brother, sister, uncle, aunt, nephew or niece. Relationships by marriage are treated as relationships by blood; relationships of half-blood are treated as relationships of whole blood; stepchildren are treated as children; and illegitimate children are treated as legitimate: s.3A(5).

It is important for practitioners to recognise that this exclusion is not as broad in its application as that relating to a resident landlord or licensor, principally because the whilst the premises must be shared with the member of the landlord's family, the landlord must also live in the same "building" (which cannot be a purpose built block of flats). The exclusion might therefore catch a lodging arrangement in a family home or someone sharing with the adult child of the landlord in the next-door semi-detached house for example.

Temporary expedient for a trespasser

A tenancy or licence is excluded if it was granted as a temporary expedient to a person who entered the premises in question or any other premises as a trespasser (whether or not, before the beginning of that tenancy or licence, another tenancy or licence to occupy the premises or any other premises had been granted to him): s.3A(6).

Holiday lettings

A tenancy or licence is excluded if it confers on the tenant or licensee the right to occupy the premises for a holiday only: s.3A(7)(a).

Other than for money or money's worth

A tenancy or licence is excluded if it is granted otherwise than for money or money's worth: s.3A(7)(b). In *West Wiltshire DC v Snelgrove* (1998) 30 HLR 57, QBD, the payment made was restricted to payment for facilities, services and food and the payee was not, therefore, a residential occupier. However, keeping the property repaired and insured had been a valuable benefit to the owner and was the quid pro quo for the licence on the facts: *Polar Park Enterprises Inc v Allason* [2007] EWHC 1088 (Ch); [2008] 1 P & CR 4.

Accommodation for asylum seekers

A tenancy or licence is excluded if it is granted in order to provide accommodation to asylum seekers and their dependents under s.4 or Part VI of the Immigration and Asylum Act 1999: s.3A(7A).

Displaced persons

A tenancy or licence is currently excluded if it is granted in order to provide accommodation under the Displaced Persons (Temporary Protection) Regulations 2005: s.3A(7C). In consequence of the revocation of these regulations as part of Brexit, this exclusion is to be repealed by the Immigration, Nationality and Asylum (EU Exit) Regulations 2019/745 Sch.3 para.1(a) from the end of the implementation period for Brexit (currently December 31, 2020).

Falls outside of "right to rent" provisions

A tenancy or licence is excluded if it is a residential tenancy agreement within the meaning of Chapter 1 of Part 3 of the Immigration Act 2014 ("IA 2014") (which broadly prevents private sector lettings to those without appropriate immigration status), and the condition in s.33D(2) of that Act is met in relation to that agreement: s.3A(7D), IA 2014.

Section 20, IA 2014 provides that a residential tenancy agreement for these purposes means a tenancy (including a lease, licence, sub-lease or sub-tenancy or any agreement for the same) which grants a right of occupation of premises for residential use, provides for payment of rent (whether or not a market rent), and is not an excluded agreement (meaning any agreement of a description for the time being specified in Sch.3: i.e., social housing, care homes, hospitals and hospices, other healthcare accommodation, hostels and refuges, accommodation from or involving local authorities, mobile homes, tied accommodation, student accommodation and long leases as defined).

The condition in s.33D(2), IA 2014 is that the Secretary of State has given one or more notices in writing to the landlord which, taken together (i) identify the occupier(s) of the premises, and (ii) state that the occupier(s) are disqualified as a result of their immigration status from occupying premises under a residential tenancy agreement.

It is important for advisors to understand that the exclusion of such occupants does not entitle a landlord to simply evict such occupants without more. Where all occupants are denied the right to rent, upon the Secretary of State giving notice to the landlord under s.33D(2), IA 2014, the landlord remains obliged to serve notice on the occupants in a prescribed form: s33D(3) IA 2014 and Sch.1, Immigration (Residential Accommodation) (Termination of Residential Tenancy Agreements) (Guidance etc.) Regulations 2016 SI 2016/1060. Upon that notice period expiring, the notice is enforcable as though an order of the High Court: s.33D(7), IA 2014. The landlord has the option to re-enter peaceably (by e.g. changing the locks) or to apply for bailiffs to evict the occupants. Again, care should be taken not to commit an offence under s.6, Criminal Law Act 1977.

The situation is different if not all the occupants of the accommodation are denied the right to rent. In those cases, the agreement pursuant to which the occupants occupy will likely fall within one of the statutory schemes for security of tenure. If it does not, it contains an implied term that "the landlord may terminate the tenancy if the premises to which it relates are occupied by an adult who is disqualified as a result of their immigration status from occupying premises under a residential tenancy agreement": s.33(1), IA 2014. In both instances, the landlord can terminate the tenancies using the proper process (Ground 10A, Sch.15, Rent Act 1977, Ground 7B, Housing Act 1988 or notice to quit for breach of the implied term). These grounds require the taking of court proceedings but, so long as the notice requirements and conditions in the grounds are met, provide that the court must make a possession order.

Licences of public authority hostels

A licence is excluded if it confers rights of occupation in a hostel (within the meaning of the Housing Act 1985, s.622), which is provided by:

- a local authority (as defined);

- an economic prosperity board established under s.88 of the Local Democracy, Economic Development and Construction Act 2009;
- a combined authority established under s.103 of that Act;
- a development corporation within the meaning of the New Towns Act 1981;
- the new towns residuary body
- an urban development corporation established by an order under section 135 of the Local Government, Planning and Land Act 1980;
- a Mayoral development corporation;
- a housing action trust established under Part III of the Housing Act 1988;
- the Regulator of Social Housing;
- the Secretary of State under s.89 of the Housing Associations Act 1985;
- a housing trust (within the meaning of the Housing Associations Act 1985) which is a charity, a private registered provider of social housing or a registered social landlord (within the meaning of the Housing Act 1985); or
- any other person who is, or who belongs to a class of person which is, specified in an order made by the Secretary of State: s.3A(8). The specified classes of persons are currently hostels provided by Royal British Legion Industries Ltd: the Protection from Eviction (Excluded Licences) (Royal British Legion Industries Ltd) (England) Order 2003/2436; the Shaftesbury Society: Protection from Eviction (Excluded Licences) (The Shaftesbury Society) Order 1999/1758; and the London Hostels Associ-

ations Ltd: Protection from Eviction (Excluded Licences) Order 1991/1943.

Section 622, Housing Act 1985 defines a *"hostel"* as a building in which is provided, for persons generally or for a class or classes of persons: (a) residential accommodation *otherwise than in separate and self-contained sets of premises*, and (b) either board or facilities for the preparation of food adequate to the needs of those persons, or both. In *Rogerson v Wigan MBC* [2004] EWHC 1677 (QB); [2005] 2 All E.R. 1000, it was held that an express term of a licence that its occupant could be required to move from one unit to another and share with a stranger meant that the accommodation was "otherwise than in separate ad self-contained sets of premises".

Application to restricted contracts

The protection of s.3, PEA 1977 applies in relation to any restricted contract within the meaning of the Rent Act 1977 which creates a licence and is entered into after the commencement of s.69 of the HA 1980; as they apply in relation to a restricted contract which creates a tenancy: s.3(2A).

Transitional arrangements for pre-HA 1988 tenancies

A tenancy (or agreement for a tenancy) entered into before the date on which the Housing Act 1988 came into force is not excluded by s.3A despite falling within the excluded categories: s.3(2C).

Death of a Rent Act statutory tenant

Section 3, PEA 1977 applies where the owner's right to recover possession arises on the death of the tenant under a statutory tenancy within the meaning of the Rent Act 1977 or the Rent (Agriculture) Act 1976: s.3(3).

Housing Act 1988, s.27

Section 27, HA 1988 was introduced to discourage landlords from unlawfully evicting Rent Act tenants so as to take advantage of the higher rents chargeable to assured tenants: see *Housing: The Government's Proposals* (White Paper, Cm.214, 1987).

This is the cause of action statistically most likely to apply in a case of unlawful eviction because it applies to such a broad spectrum of tenures, from contractual licensees to secure and assured tenants and s.3 and 3A exclude many types of tenancy and licence from the protection of s.3, PEA 1977.

It provides as follows:

> *"(1) This section applies if, at any time after 9th June 1988, a landlord (in this section referred to as "the landlord in default") or any person acting on behalf of the landlord in default unlawfully deprives the residential occupier of any premises of his occupation of the whole or part of the premises.*
>
> *(2) This section also applies if, at any time after 9th June 1988, a landlord (in this section referred to as "the landlord in default") or any person acting on behalf of the landlord in default—*
>
> > *(a) attempts unlawfully to deprive the residential occupier of any premises of his occupation of the whole or part of the premises, or*
> >
> > *(b) knowing or having reasonable cause to believe that the conduct is likely to cause the residential occupier of any premises —*
> >
> > > *(i) to give up his occupation of the premises or any part thereof, or*
> > >
> > > *(ii) to refrain from exercising any right or pursuing any remedy in respect of the premises or any part thereof,*

does acts likely to interfere with the peace or comfort of the residential occupier or members of his household, or persistently withdraws or withholds services reasonably required for the occupation of the premises as a residence, and, as a result, the residential occupier gives up his occupation of the premises as a residence.

(3) Subject to the following provisions of this section, where this section applies, the landlord in default shall, by virtue of this section, be liable to pay to the former residential occupier, in respect of his loss of the right to occupy the premises in question as his residence, damages assessed on the basis set out in section 28 below."

The section covers three discrete issues: first, unlawful eviction (s.27(1)); secondly, attempts to evict: s.27(2)(a); and, thirdly, conduct designed to result in, and which does result in, a tenant giving up occupation of premises as a residence: s.27(2)(b).

Notably, the section does not include a corresponding right to claim for an injunction (which e.g. ss.3 and 3A, PHA 1997 provide in the context of harassment).

<u>"Residential occupier"</u>

"Residential occupier" means the same as in s.1, PEA 1977: s.27(9), i.e., a person occupying the premises as a residence, whether under a contract or by virtue of any enactment or rule of law giving him the right to remain in occupation or restricting the right of any other person to recover possession of the premises. As such, it applies to protected tenants under the Rent Act 1977, secure tenants under HA 1985 as well as assured and assured shorthold tenants and licensees under HA 1988.

The reference to "by virtue of any enactment" extends to s.3, PEA 1977 (i.e. the need to obtain a court order) and so the fact a licence may have ended does not mean a person can be evicted. Moreover, once a possession order is obtained, the landlord is obliged to use bailiffs to carry out the eviction: *Haniff v Robinson (1992) 26 HLR 386, CA.* In short, if a landlord is required to take court proceedings to evict an occupant, he must exhaust the county court procedure. It must surely follow that where there is room for doubt as to whether a person remains a residential occupier of the premises a landlord should err on the side of caution and obtain a possession order and apply for a bailiff's warrant.

"Landlord"

"Landlord", in relation to a residential occupier, means the person who, but for the occupier's right to occupy, would be entitled to occupation of the premises as well as any superior landlord under whom that person derives title: s.27(9).

Landlord's agents

As stated above, it is only the landlord who can be liable under s.27 and is so liable for the acts or omissions of his agent. Liability under this section therefore does not attach to an agent acting on a landlord's behalf: *Sampson v Wilson* [1996] Ch. 39, 29 HLR 18, CA.

Liability

Any liability arising by s.27(3) is in tort and in addition to any other liability whether in tort, contract or otherwise, but damages cannot be awarded for both in respect of the same loss: s.27(4) and (5). In essence, this puts a claimant to election as to the method by which his damages are calculated.

Of particular relevance to this decision will be the extent to which any reinstatement will deprive the tenant of damages under s.28.

Liability extinguished on reinstatement

Crucially, from a practitioner's point of view, no liability for damages assessed in accordance with s.28, HA 1988 arises under s.27(3) if a former residential occupier "*is* reinstated" as a residential occupier, whether as a result of a court order or by the owner of their own volition, before the date on which proceedings to enforce the liability are finally disposed of (including determination or abandonment of any appeal or expiry of the time limit for appealing): s.27(6).

A temporary return is not sufficient for reinstatement: *Mehta v Royal Bank of Scotland Plc* (2000) 32 H.L.R. 45. In *Tagro v Cafane* [1991] 1 W.L.R. 378 there had been no reinstatement where the property had been wrecked and the lock did not work, the upshot of this decision being that reinstatement has to be physically possible.

The effect of being unable to pursue reinstatement was felt keenly in *Smith v Khan* [2018] EWCA Civ 1137; [2018] H.L.R. 31. So far as relevant to the question of readmittance, the Defendant's ("K") husband rented a flat for the family for a fixed term due to end on 30.6.15. Owing to rent arrears accruing, he left the flat in March 2015 to find work, leaving K there. On 1.4.15, the landlord gave K notice to end the tenancy which was defective. K sought advice from the Citizens Advice Bureau which wrote to the landlord informing him the notice was invalid and he needed to obtain a court order for possession. On 15.4.15, whilst K was away from the flat, the landlord changed the locks. K issued a claim for damages and an injunction to be readmitted to the flat. On 18.5.15, an order for readmittance was granted but by that time, the landlord had re-let the flat.

In finding that damages were only payable from the date of the eviction until the expiry of the fixed term (76 days in total), the Court of Appeal held that by that date, the claimant had elected not to pursue her claim for reinstatement and had collected her belongings; by 30.6.15, both the claimant and her husband must have accepted that they would not regain possession of the flat and that their occupation of it as an only or principal home had ceased; and accordingly, since there was no contractual right under the tenancy agreement to a further lease and neither of them remained in possession paying rent, no statutory periodic tenancy arose under s.5(2), Housing Act 1988 and the tenancy came to an end at the expiry of the fixed term.

This is a somewhat surprising outcome given the incentive it provides for a landlord of a tenancy still within its fixed term to "cap" exposure to damages by reletting the premises as quickly as possible and in any event prior to the expiry of that fixed term. Of equal concern is the approach the court took to assessing the measure of damage at common law and this is considered in more detail in Chapter 6.

It is advisable to claim for reinstatement in any case where there is a prospect of it being ordered and the client feels safe to return. Delay only serves to aid the landlord's reletting of the property in order to defeat such a claim (which operates on equitable principles analogous to an injunction). It is *critical* for practitioners faced with an unlawful eviction from a property let on a fixed-term tenancy which is yet to expire to highlight the urgency of the application for reinstatement to the court.

Defence

In proceedings to enforce a liability arising by virtue of s.27(3), it is a defence for the defendant to prove that he believed, and had reasonable cause to believe:

a) that the residential occupier had ceased to reside in the premises in question at the time when he was evicted or, as the case may be, when the attempt was made or the acts were done as a result of which he gave up his occupation of those premises; or

b) that, where the liability would otherwise arise by virtue only of the doing of acts or the withdrawal or withholding of services, he had reasonable grounds for doing the acts or withdrawing or withholding the services in question.

OTHER COMMON LAW TORTS

Trespass to land

In the context of unlawful eviction, a trespass to land occurs *inter alia* where a landlord retakes possession of the premises unlawfully. The trespass occurs when a landlord, in the absence of the tenant's permission, (i) enters the premises or (ii) remains on them having had a reasonable opportunity to leave: see generally Clerk & Lindsell on Torts (2018), 22nd ed. at Chapter 19.

In order to sue for trespass, the occupant must have an interest in the land. An unlawful eviction is therefore a trespass to land if the landlord re-takes possession before the tenancy has ended: *Smith v Khan*, above.

In a harassment case, trespass to land may include posting material through the letterbox or daubing graffiti on the premises.

In a claim for unlawful eviction, trespass should invariably be pleaded alongside breach of the covenant for quiet enjoyment in order to ensure that general damages for distress and inconvenience as well as aggravated and exemplary damages can be claimed.

Nuisance

Harassment is capable of amounting to a private nuisance if it interferes with an occupant's ordinary and reasonable enjoyment of property where he is lawfully present: *Khorasandjian v Bush* [1993] Q.B. 727, where harassing telephone calls were made to someone's home. This decision was overruled in part by *Hunter v Canary Wharf Ltd* [1997] AC 684, (1997) 30 H.L.R. 409, HL which reaffirmed that a cause of action in private nuisance would not lie unless the claimant had either title to the land or (if he could not prove title) was in exclusive occupation of it: *Foster v Warblington Urban DC* [1906] 1 K.B. 648.

In context, a tenant would be able to sue for nuisance caused by harassing conduct but a bare licensee who occupied the premises with the tenant such as a family member could not. A trespasser in adverse possession is able to sue in private nuisance for harassing conduct. The problem with the restricted availability of this cause of action is addressed largely by the Protection from Harassment Act 1997 (see Chapter 5).

Wrongful interference with/trespass to goods

In cases where an occupant's belongings have been interfered with (whether removed from drawers, placed in bags, left outside the premises or placed in storage) a claim for wrongful interference with goods (which includes trespass to goods and/or conversion) will be available pursuant to s.3, Torts (Interference with Goods) Act 1977.

Relief under T(IG)A 1977 comprises an order for delivery of the goods to the claimant or a person appointed by the court and consequential damages or for damages in lieu of delivery: s.3(2). An application for interim relief in proceedings for wrongful interference can be made in the County Court: s.4, T(IG)A 1977.

This cause of action is commonly pleaded in cases of unlawful eviction where a person's belongings have been taken or damaged in the course of the eviction. It generally gives rise to a claim for special damages arising from the eviction (the measure of such loss being the market value of the goods at the time they were taken). Thus, when pleading a claim for trespass to or conversion of goods where damages in lieu of return are sought, it is important to have assessed the value of loss in the early stages, not least because that value (i) will inform a client's position for the purposes of compliance with the pre-action protocol, and (ii) will provide a basis for the figure included in the statement of value under CPR r.16.3.

Advisors should not neglect to plead consequential losses arising from the interference such as the cost of hiring replacement goods or additional costs incurred to travel to work from a temporary address as well as damages for distress and inconvenience. The latter may outstrip the market value of many sentimental items such as photographs, letters or gifts.

Others

There are other causes of action which may be relevant in any given case but which are beyond the scope of this book. In particular, where violence, threats or intimidation are involved in an unlawful eviction or harassment case, the torts of assault, verbal abuse and intimidation will be relevant in addition to the causes of action referred to above.

Caravan Sites Act 1968/Mobile Homes (Wales) Act 2013

Also, by s.3, Caravan Sites Act 1968, comparable protection to that in s.3, PEA 1977 is provided to park home residents. It is unclear whether similar provisions under s.42, Mobile Homes (Wales) Act 2013 give rise to a civil cause of action.

POINTS TO NOTE

- There is significant conflicting comment on whether ss.2 and 3, PEA 1977 provide an actionable tort compounded by the recent decision in *Smith v Khan* (above). However, close scrutiny of the decisions suggests that the comment is either *obiter* or based on the absence of full argument. The point still appears to be governed by the decision in *Warder v Cooper* (above), i.e. that s.3, PEA 1977 gives rise to the civil cause of action. To avoid any dispute, a claim should invariably plead trespass alongside any breach of statutory duty.

- The fact an occupant occupies mixed-use premises does not prevent a claim for unlawful eviction being brought under s.2, PEA 1977: *Pirabakan* (above).

- It is a common error to plead a claim for unlawful eviction in reliance on s.3, PEA 1977 for a statutorily protected tenancy (which remains statutorily protected unless surrendered, ended by a tenant notice to quit or the tenant is evicted pursuant to a court order: s.5(1), HA 1988). Section 3, PEA 1977 does not apply to such tenancies and the claim should be based on s.27(1), HA 1988. Conversely, if a statutorily protected tenant served a notice to quit (thus ending the tenancy on the quit date) but then refused to vacate the premises and was evicted without a court order, the claim would be under s.3, PEA 1977.

- All of the various causes of action can present confusion for practitioners regarding which should be pleaded and relied upon. In summary, where a claim is brought in respect of an unlawful eviction where the tenancy is statutorily protected, the claim should include a cause of action for breach of quiet enjoyment (contract) and trespass (tort) as well as s.27 (tort) (pending any reinstatement which may occur).

- Section 27, HA 1988 does not permit a claimant to claim for an interim injunction (albeit it specifically refers to reinstatement to the premises) and that relief should be sought on the back of another cause of action (i.e. breach of covenant or trespass).

- In cases where a tenancy is not statutorily protected then s.3, PEA 1977 should be pleaded. If there is a dispute about whether or not the tenancy or licence is statutorily protected, then both should be pleaded in the alternative.

- Exclusion from s.3, PEA 1977 does not preclude a claim for harassment (see Chapter 5) and a landlord should also ensure no offences under s.6, CLA 1977 are committed (see Chapter 4).

- A claim for trespass to land and/or goods should always be contemplated in cases of unlawful eviction.

- If goods have been removed, tampered with or damaged, a claim for trespass to goods should also be brought under s.4, T(IG)A 1977. Ascertaining the value of goods damaged or converted is necessary and the measure of such damage is calculated by the market value of the goods at the time they are damaged or converted.

CHAPTER FOUR
UNLAWFUL EVICTION (CRIMINAL OFFENCES AND OTHER REMEDIES)

This chapter looks at the criminal offence of unlawful eviction. Those offences relating to harassment designed to result in a residential occupier giving up occupation of their home are dealt with in Chapter 5. It is less common for private prosecutions to be brought against landlords or licensors in respect of criminal offences arising from unlawful eviction, primarily because Magistrates' Courts tend to be reluctant to allow them to take up court time and costs are not recoverable even if a private prosecution is successful. The main circumstances in which a landlord would be prosecuted for such offences is where a complaint is made to a local authority which elects to take action (ordinarily this would happen as part of a broader strategy to improve housing standards within its area). The availability of banning orders might be shown to provide a renewed incentive to prosecute those landlords who are particularly unscrupulous in their operations.

CRIMINAL OFFENCES

Protection from Eviction Act 1977, s.1(2)

By s.1(2), PEA 1977:

> *"If any person unlawfully deprives the residential occupier of any premises of his occupation of the premises or any part thereof, or attempts to do so, he shall be guilty of an offence unless he proves that he believed, and had reasonable cause to believe, that the residential occupier had ceased to reside in the premises..."*

"Unlawfully"

Whether a residential occupant is "unlawfully" deprived of occupation is broadly dictated by the scheme of the Act. Both ss.2 and 3 of the PEA 1977 make eviction in prescribed circumstances unlawful: s.2 where it states that "where any premises are let as a dwelling on a lease which is subject to a right of re-entry or forfeiture it *shall not be lawful* to enforce that right otherwise than by proceedings in the court while any person is lawfully residing in the premises or part of them"; and s.3 which, in the context of a letting of a dwelling which is not statutorily protected or excluded under s.3A, provides it *shall not be lawful* for an owner to enforce against an occupier, otherwise than by proceedings in the court, the right to recover possession of the premises.

In addition, the commission of a tort would amount to an unlawful act e.g. any deprivation which also amounted to a trespass (such as not permitting an occupant entry) or a nuisance (such as creating noise or smells which had the effect of forcing a person to leave the premises) as would any breach of contract.

"Premises"

This is given a broad meaning: *Thurrock UDC v Shina* (1972) 23 P & CR 205, QBD; *Uratemp Ventures Ltd v Collins* (above) which has been held to apply to rooms with shared facilities and even caravans in some circumstances (in situ for 10 years and not easily moved): *Norton v Knowles* [1969] 1 QB 572, QBD.

Deprivation of occupation

Not every locking out amounts to an eviction for the purposes of s.1(1). In *R v Yuthiwattana (Helen)* (1985) 80 Cr App R 55; (1984) 16 HLR 49, one day and one night were not sufficient to amount to deprivation of the tenant's occupation of the room (albeit were sufficient to amount to harassment in breach of s.1(3) – see Chapter 4). In reaching this decision, the Court of Appeal had regard to (and rowed back somewhat) from the observations of Lord Evershed M.R. in *Crown Lands Commissioners v Page* [1960] 2 QB 274 where it was held that eviction "must be of a permanent character". In *Yuthiwattana*, Kerr LJ held:

> *"In our view "permanency" goes too far. For instance, if the owner of the premises unlawfully tells the occupier that he must leave the premises for some period, it may be of months or weeks, and then excludes him from the premises, or does anything else with the result that the occupier effectively has to leave the premises and find other accommodation, then it would in our view be open to a jury to convict the owner under sub-s (2) on the ground that he had unlawfully deprived the occupier of his occupation. On the other hand, cases which are more properly described as "locking out" or not admitting the occupier on one or even more isolated occasions, so that in effect he continues to be allowed to occupy the premises but is then unable to enter, seem to us to fall appropriately under sub-s (3)(a) or (b), which deal with acts of harassment."*

The reasoning in *Yuthiwattana* was applied in *Costelloe v Camden LBC* [1986] Crim. L.R. 249, DC. Mr Costelloe had let two rooms of his flat to two women. He told Miss B that she was to move out by May 6. He had told Miss S. to move out by May 13. On May 9, he refused to allow either woman to enter the flat but offered, an hour later (and after police intervention) to allow Miss S to return for the night. Miss S collected her property and left. Mr Costelloe was charged under s.1(2) for Miss S' unlawful eviction and was convicted in the Magistrate's Court. He appealed unsuccessfully to the Crown Court which stated a case to the High Court. In allowing the appeal, the High Court held that *Yuthiwattana* made it clear that if a residential occupier is excluded from premises, apparently permanently, in circumstances in which he thinks he has been so excluded and it appears to be the landlord's intention to exclude the occupier permanently, but there is for any reason a re-admission, such a case could nevertheless come within s.1(2), PEA 1977 even though the absence was for a short time only. Nonetheless, there had been no finding as to whether Miss S was being evicted only for a short time. In view of the lapse of time it would not be appropriate to send the case back for further facts to be found; the proper course was to assume that the Court would have found the exclusion was temporary.

Woolf J observed that the short reports of *Yuthiwattana* gave the impression that *the period* of the exclusion was critical which was wrong. The proper test was, "what was the nature of the exclusion; [and] was it designed to evict the occupier?" If so, the conduct fell within s.1(2), PEA 1977.

The key point to take from the above is that when determining whether an occupant has been "deprived of occupation" it is not enough to simply look at the amount of time a person was out of the premises. The key is to establish whether the landlord's actions which resulted in the exclusion of the occupier were designed to evict him.

"Residential occupier"

Section 1(1) defines *"residential occupier"*, in relation to any premises, as a person occupying the premises as a residence, whether under a contract or by virtue of any enactment or rule of law giving him the right to remain in occupation or restricting the right of any other person to recover possession of the premises. This covers an incredibly broad spectrum of potential occupiers including statutorily protected tenancies, leaseholders, those who cannot be evicted without a court order pursuant to s.3, PEA 1977, licensees and even some trespassers if in adverse possession (which is a complex area in itself and beyond the scope of this book).

Offence

A person guilty of an offence under s.1(2), PEA 1977 is liable on summary conviction, to a fine not exceeding the prescribed sum or to imprisonment for a term not exceeding six months or to both; and on conviction on indictment, to a fine or to imprisonment for a term not exceeding two years or to both: s.1(4), PEA 1977.

Nothing in s.1(2), PEA 1977 prevents civil proceedings being taken against an offender: s.1(5), PEA 1977.

As the offence is triable either way, there is no requirement for an information to be laid before the Magistrates' Court within six months of the offence: s.127(2), Magistrates' Courts Act 1980.

Penalties for the offence are notoriously low compared to damages awards in civil proceedings. By way of example, in a case in the Oxford Magistrates' Court and prosecuted by Oxford City Council, a fine of £180 was imposed for an unlawful eviction and £300 for a campaign of harassment. Between April and June 2014, the offender – along with family members – had repeatedly threatened the tenant with violence and then locked him out of his home by changing the lock to the front door.

It is fair to say that the introduction of banning orders (which can, if properly enforced, seriously interfere with a landlord's ability to generate property-related income) will serve as much greater deterrent than the paltry amounts awarded by way of compensation in criminal proceedings to those unlawfully evicted. The fact remains that the time and cost incurred in pursuing a prosecution, coupled with the uncertainty of outcome and the fact that a victim would still have to bring a civil cause of action to get anywhere close to adequate compensation for the loss suffered, is likely to result in a slow uptake by local authorities.

<u>Companies</u>

A company can be guilty of an offence under s.1(2), PEA 1977 committed with the consent or connivance of, or to be attributable to any neglect on the part of, any director, manager or secretary or other similar officer of the body corporate or any person who was purporting to act in any such capacity. In such circumstances both the company and the individual concerned are guilty of the offence: s.1(6), PEA 1977.

<u>Defence</u>

It is a defence to prove that the accused believed, and had reasonable cause to believe, that the occupier had ceased to reside in the premises. This creates a legal burden on the defendant to establish his or her reasonable belief on the balance of probabilities (the imposition of which was held to be compatible with European Convention on Human Rights, art 6(2): *Attorney General's Reference (No.1 of 2004)* [2004] 1 W.L.R. 2111). Whether the accused held that belief and whether it was reasonable for him to hold it are matters for the jury to decide: *R. v Davidson-Acres* (1980) Crim LR 50, CA.

Criminal Law Act 1977

By s.6(1), CLA 1977, any person who, without lawful authority, uses or threatens violence for the purpose of securing entry into any premises for himself or for any other person is guilty of an offence, provided that there is someone present on those premises at the time who is opposed to the entry which the violence is intended to secure; and the person using or threatening the violence knows that that is the case.

By s.6(4) CLA 1977, whether the violence in question is directed against the person or against property; and the purpose of the entry which the violence is intended to secure are irrelevant matters.

There is an exception to the above offence: namely where the person threatening violence is a displaced residential occupier or a protected intending occupier of the premises in question or any person acting on their behalf: s.6(1A), CLA 1977. If the accused adduces sufficient evidence that he was a displaced residential occupier or a protected intending occupier (or was acting on behalf of such an occupier) then he is presumed to be (or be acting on behalf of) such an occupier and the burden of showing he was not shifts to the prosecution: s.6(1A), CLA 1977.

Subject to this exception, the fact that a person has any interest in or right to possession or occupation of any premises does not constitute lawful authority for the use or threat of violence by him or anyone else for the purpose of securing his entry to the premises: s.6(2), CLA 1977. A person guilty of an offence under s.6(1), CLA 1977 is liable on summary conviction to imprisonment for a term not exceeding six months or to a fine not exceeding level 5 on the standard scale or to both: s.6(5), CLA 1977.

As the offence is summary only, an information must be laid before the Magistrates' Court within six months of the offence: s.127(2), Magistrates' Courts Act 1980.

Displaced residential occupier

A "displaced residential occupier" is any person (except a trespasser) who was occupying any premises as a residence immediately before being excluded from occupation by anyone who entered those premises, or any access to those premises, as a trespasser, so long as he continues to be excluded from occupation of the premises by the original trespasser or by any subsequent trespasser: s.12, CLA 1977.

Protected intended occupier

A "protected intended occupier" is, in broad terms, an individual who requires the premises for his own occupation but is prevented from taking up occupation by a trespasser. The individual must be (i) a freeholder or a leaseholder (whose lease has at least two years to run) with a sworn statement to this effect; (ii) a tenant or licensee of a local authority, a registered provider of social housing or a registered social landlord with a certificate from the landlord to this effect; (iii) any other tenant or licensee of a freeholder or a leaseholder (whose lease has at least two years to run) with a sworn statement to this effect: s.12A, CLA 1977.

OTHER REMEDIES

Rent repayment orders

The First-tier Tribunal (Property Chamber) ("FTT") has power to make a rent repayment order ("RRO") against a landlord in England who has committed an offence under *inter alia* PEA 1977 s.1(2) (as well as s.1(3) and (3A), see Chapter 4, and/or breach of a banning order, see below), where the offence took place on or after 6.4.17: s.40, Housing and Planning Act 2016.

A landlord for the above purposes includes a superior landlord: *Goldsbrough v CA Property Management Ltd* [2019] UKUT 311 (LC); [2020] H.L.R. 18.

A tenant or a local authority may apply for such an order within 12 months of the offence: s.41, HPA 2016. In the absence of exceptional circumstances (see s.46), a tenant will be able to recover an amount of rent paid during the period of 12 months ending with the date of the offence, not including any benefit element: s.44, HPA 2016. The benefit element is repaid to the local authority on its application: s.45(3), HPA 2016. In determining the amount, the tribunal must take into account, the conduct of the landlord and the tenant, the financial circumstances of the landlord, and whether the landlord has at any time been convicted of an offence under Chapter 4 (as for which see s.40(3), HPA 2016): s.44(4), HPA 2016.

In *Vadamalayan v Stewart* [2020] UKUT 0183 (LC), Judge Cooke held that when deciding "an amount" for the purposes of s.44, the starting point was the full amount of rent for the period in question and there was no longer[1] any basis for repaying to the tenant only the extent of the landlord's profit (accounting for any utilities the tenant uses for which the landlord pays).

The power does not depend on a conviction but in the absence of one, the applicant will need to prove his case beyond reasonable doubt. *Opara v Olasemo* [2020] UKUT 96 (LC), provides a useful illustration of how the burden of proof operates practically in the context of RRO applications involving an unlawful eviction. In *Opara*, Mr Opara appealed against a decision of the FTT refusing his application for an RRO. The FTT had not been satisfied to the criminal standard that the respondent, Ms Olasemo, had committed the offences of unlawful

1 It had previously been the understood (in the context of ss.73 and 74, Housing Act 2004) that the amount was limited to the landlord's profit: *Parker v Waller* [2012] UKUT 301 (LC).

eviction and/or managing a HMO without a licence.[2] Mr Opara contended that the FTT should have been so satisfied, and did not take proper account of the evidence before it.

Regarding the unlawful eviction, the FTT was persuaded that the respondent had not changed the lock on the door of Mr Opara's room (it having been suggested in legal submissions that the lock might have broken or might have stuck because it had just been painted). It was suggested that there were some "reasonably friendly" messages between the parties about Mr Opara picking up his belongings; his belongings had not been thrown out into the street and might plausibly have been moved by the decorators; and Mr Opara "did not make any endeavours whether legally or practically to get a locksmith along to gain access to his room." The FTT considered it at least *possible* that Ms Olameso's case was correct: that there was no real problem with the lock, that Mr Opara had mis-read the situation; and that Ms Olasemo's text messages were not intended as a notice to quit and he was welcome to move back in. The FTT therefore concluded that whilst it would have been satisfied on the *balance of probabilities* that the respondent had "procured Mr Opara to vacate so that she could move herself in and bring her HMO problems to a close", it could not be so satisfied *beyond reasonable doubt* and the application failed.

On appeal to the Upper Tribunal (Lands Chamber), Judge Cooke said the following about the FFT's approach (at [46]):

> *"The FTT in its decision in this case was, I think, over-cautious about making inferences from evidence. For a matter to be proved to the criminal standard it must be proved 'beyond reasonable doubt'; it does not have to be proved 'beyond any doubt at all'. At the start of a criminal trial the judge warns the jury not to speculate about evidence that they have not heard, but also tells them that it is permissible for them to draw inferences from the evidence that they accept. In this case there were obvious inferences to be drawn from the evidence, both about the eviction and about the circumstances of*

2 Another prescribed offence giving rise to an entitlement to apply for an RRO: s.40(3), Housing and Planning Act 2016.

> *the other tenants. It may be that the FTT lost sight of those inferences and set the bar of proof too high. I say that in the hope that it is of assistance for the future."*

The decision in *Salva v Singh-Potiwal* [2019] UKUT 307 (LC) is a salutary reminder that the offences in s.1(2), (3) and (3A) are separate and distinct. Ms Salva appealed against the FFT's refusal to make an RRO, the Tribunal having found, amongst other things, that there was no unlawful eviction under s.1(2), PEA 1977, because Ms Salva had left the property voluntarily after her landlord gave notice to vacate via text message. Ms Salva contended that she had been harassed which ultimately led to her quitting the property. The FTT had not found this offence proved either. Mr Salva did not appeal the FTT's finding on harassment. Judge Elizabeth Cooke allowed the appeal on unrelated grounds but, in finding the FFT's decision regarding the unlawful eviction was correct, held that the fact she may have left as a result of harassment was not an issue on appeal.

Insofar as it is contended that a landlord's actions have resulted in a residential occupier ceasing to occupy his accommodation but those circumstances are disputed and/or do not clearly suggest an eviction took place, then the harassment offence(s) in s.1(3) and/or (3A) ought to be included alongside the eviction offence in s.1(2), PEA 1997. See also the dicta of Glidewell L.J. in *Costelloe* (above) "a prosecutor in doubt as to whether the facts constituted an offence under section 1(2) or section 1(3) (harassment) may charge the offences in the alternative".

Banning orders

Since 6.4.18, a local authority has been able to apply to the First-tier Tribunal for a banning order against a person who or body corporate (and any officer thereof) which has been convicted of a banning order offence which took place after that date: s.15(1) and (2), Housing and Planning Act 2016 ("HPA 2016").

Practitioners are referred to the "Banning Order Offences under the Housing and Planning Act 2016, Guidance for Local Housing Authorities", April 2018 for guidance on how local authorities are expected to approach the new area.

The offences

The offences in respect of which a banning order can be sought are:

- An offence under s.12, Tenant Fees Act 2019: s.14(5), HPA 2016 (requiring a person to make a prohibited payment within five years of a penalty having been imposed for a prior breach).

- An offence under s.1(2), (3) or (3A), PEA 1977: s.14(3), HPA 2016 and reg.3, Housing and Planning Act 2016 (Banning Order Offences) Regulations 2018 (SI 2018/216).

- An offence under s.6(1), CLA 1977, unless the sentence imposed on the person convicted of the offence ("the offender") is an absolute discharge or a conditional discharge: *ibid*, reg.3(a).

- An offence under s.2, PHA 1977, if:

    i. the offence was committed against or in collusion with a tenant occupying any housing (or another person occupying that housing with the tenant) or the offence was committed at or in relation to that housing;

    ii. at the time the offence was committed, the offender was the residential landlord or property agent of that housing or an officer of a body corporate who was the residential landlord or property agent of that housing; and

    iii. the offender was sentenced for the offence in the Crown Court: *ibid*, reg.3(c).

The application

The First-tier Tribunal can apply for a banning order against a person if that person was a residential landlord or property agent at the time the offence was committed: s.16, HPA 2016.

Notice and representations

Before applying for a banning order, the authority must give the person a notice of intended proceedings:

- informing the person that the authority is proposing to apply for a banning order and explaining why,
- stating the length of each proposed ban, and
- inviting the person to make representations within a period specified in the notice of not less than 28 days ("the notice period"): s.15(3), HPA 2016.

The authority must consider any representations made during the notice period: s.15(4), HPA 2016.

The authority must wait until the notice period has ended before applying for a banning order: s.15(5), HPA 2016.

Limitation

A notice of intended proceedings may not be given after the end of the period of 6 months beginning with the day on which the person was convicted of the offence to which the notice relates: s.15(6), HPA 2016.

The application is made on First-tier Tribunal (Property Chamber) Form BN1.

The order

A banning order bans a landlord from:

- letting housing in England;
- engaging in English letting agency work;
- engaging in English property management work; or
- doing two or more of the above: s.14, HPA 2016.

Additionally, a banning order may include provision banning the person against whom it is made from being involved in any body corporate that carries out an activity that the person is banned by the order from carrying out: s.18(1), HPA 2016. For this purpose, a person is "involved" in a body corporate if the person acts as an officer of the body corporate or directly or indirectly takes part in or is concerned in the management of the body corporate: s.18(2), HPA 2016.

Considerations for the Tribunal

In deciding whether to make a banning order against a person, and in deciding what order to make, the Tribunal must consider:

(a) the seriousness of the offence of which the person has been convicted,

(b) any previous convictions that the person has for a banning order offence,

(c) whether the person is or has at any time been included in the database of rogue landlords and property agents, and

(d) the likely effect of the banning order on the person and anyone else who may be affected by the order" s.16(4), HPA 2016.

A banning order must specify the length of each ban imposed by the order which cannot be less than 12 months: s.17(1) and (2), HPA 2016. The order can contain exceptions covering some or all of the period ordered, and the exceptions themselves can be made subject to conditions: s.17(3), HPA 2016. Examples of circumstances where an exception may be appropriate include cases where there are existing tenancies and the landlord does not have the power to bring them to an immediate end, or where there is a need to allow letting agents to wind down current business: s.17(4), HPA 2016.

Power to require information

Section 19, HPA 2016 gives a local authority power to require a person to provide specified information for the purpose of enabling the authority to decide whether to apply for a banning order against the person. A failure to comply with such a requirement or the knowing or reckless provision of false information is an offence punishable by fine.

Anti-avoidance provisions

A person who is subject to a banning order that includes a ban on letting may not make an unauthorised transfer of an estate in land to a prohibited person and, if they do, the disposal is void: s.27(1) and (2), HPA 2016. A transfer is "unauthorised" unless it is authorised by the First-tier Tribunal on an application by the person who is subject to the banning order: s.27(3), HPA 2016. A prohibited person is someone associated with the landlord,[3] a business partner,[4] a person associated with the landlord's business partner, a company where any of the afore-

3 "Associated" carried a specific meaning derived from s.178, HA 1996 and includes spouses, civil partners, current or former fiancées, cohabitants or former cohabitants, people sharing a household, a relative (as defined) and co-parents (including parents of adopted children).

4 "Business partner" means the same as in s.34(5), Deregulation Act 2015 namely, a person who is a director, secretary or other officer of a company of which the landlord is also a director, secretary or other officer or in which he holds a shareholding or other financial interest (and visa-versa), an employee or employer of the landlord and a partner.

mentioned people is an officer, a company where the landlord has a shareholding or other interest or, if the landlord is a company, any other company that shares an officer with the landlord: s.27(4), HPA 2016.

Penalties on breach

By s.21, HPA 2016, breach of a banning order is a criminal offence which the police or a local authority can prosecute.

A person guilty of the offence is liable on summary conviction to imprisonment for a period not exceeding six months (for so long as s.281(5), Criminal Justice Act 2003 has not been brought into force and 51 weeks thereafter)[5] or to a fine or to both: s.21(2), HPA 2016. If the breach continues after conviction, the person commits a further offence and is liable on summary conviction to a fine not exceeding one-tenth of level 2 on the standard scale (currently £50) for each day or part of a day on which the breach continues. It is a defence to show that the person had a reasonable excuse for the continued breach: s.21(5), HPA 2016.

Where an offence under s.21, HPA 2016, committed by a body corporate, is proved to have been committed with the consent or connivance of, or to be attributable to any neglect on the part of, an officer of a body corporate, the officer as well as the body corporate commits the offence and is liable to be proceeded against and punished accordingly: s.22(1), HPA 2016. The same approach applies where the affairs of a body corporate are managed by its members, as if the member were an officer of the body corporate: s.22(2), HPA 2016.
This is not the only sanction which applies to such a breach.

- The local authority can impose a civil penalty of up to £30,000 *as an alternative to prosecution* (for a fresh penalty for each six-month period of continuing breach): s.23, HPA 2016. Schedule

5 As at the time of writing, s.281, Criminal Justice Act 2003 has yet to be brought into force.

1, HPA 2016 deals with the procedure for imposing such a penalty as well as appeals and enforcement of the same.

- The local authority cannot grant an HMO licence to a person against whom a banning order is in force and who owns an estate or interest in the house or part of it and is a lessor or licensor of the house or part: s.64, HA 2004 (as amended). It must revoke a licence already granted if
    - the licence holder becomes subject to a banning order, or
    - if a banning order is made against a person who owns an estate or interest in the house or part of it and is a lessor or licensor of the house or part: s.70A, HA 2004.
- The local authority can apply for a management order, in respect of an HMO, in order to protect the health, safety or welfare of residents: s.25 and Sch.3, HPA 2016.
- In addition, a local authority or a tenant (or licensee of the landlord) can apply to a First-tier Tribunal for an RRO where a landlord has breached a banning order.

Status of tenancies granted in breach of a banning order

A tenant who is granted a tenancy by a landlord who is a subject to a banning order has a legal tenancy: s.24, HPA 2016. Thus, the landlord must follow the lawful procedure for bringing that tenancy to an end. Any actual or attempted eviction in order to avoid or mitigate a sanction for breach would be unlawful.

Revocation and variation

A person against whom a banning order is made may apply to the First-tier Tribunal for an order under this section revoking or varying the order: s.20(1), HPA 2016. Interestingly, there is no equivalent provision for a local authority to apply to revoke or vary and order.

If the banning order was made on the basis of one or more convictions all of which are overturned on appeal, the First-tier Tribunal must revoke the banning order: s.20(2), HPA 2016, but if only some of several convictions are overturned on appeal, the Tribunal has a discretion to vary or revoke the banning order: s.20(3), HPA 2016.

If one or more convictions on which a banning order was based become spent under the Rehabilitation of Offenders Act 1974, the Tribunal may vary or revoke the banning order: s.20(4). The power to vary under s.20(3) and (4), HPA 2016 may be used to add new exceptions to a ban or to vary the banned activities, the length of a ban, or existing exceptions to a ban.

Database of rogue landlords

Where a banning order offence occurs, a local authority has a discretion to include that person in the database for the period specified in the notice served under s.31[6]: s.30, HPA 2016. Where a banning order is made, the local authority is subject to a duty to include the person against whom the banning order is made (if they have not already been included under s.30) for so long as it remains in force: s.29, HPA 2016.

POINTS TO NOTE

- **There are several offences relevant to unlawful eviction but in terms of the act of eviction itself, s.1(2) is of paramount importance.**

6 Requirement to provide a decision notice to a person prior to entering them on the database. The notice must specify the period for which the person's entry will be maintained, such period to be not less than two years.

- As with any prosecution, the task of the prosecuting authority and the defence is to ensure that each element of the offence has been scrutinised exactly. Particular attention is required when issues of the length of exclusion arise (e.g. where a tenant is readmitted without the need for a court order), and where the defence of reasonable belief is raised (which carries with it the usual problems of demonstrating evidentially both the subjective and objective element).

- A conviction now carries with it more than the mere risk of imprisonment or a fine and any reputational damage. Rent repayment orders, banning orders and being entered on the database of rogue landlords all give an incentive to comply with the law, principally because they serve to hit unscrupulous landlords where it hurts: their profit margin.

CHAPTER FIVE
HARASSMENT (CIVIL AND CRIMINAL REMEDIES)

There are both criminal offences and civil remedies relating to harassment, some of which cover harassment by any person (Protection from Eviction Act 1977 and Protection from Harassment Act 1977, s.1(1)), some of which are specific to the landlord and tenant relationship (contract and s.1(3A), PEA 1977) and one of which relates specifically to harassment suffered in the course of occupation of a home (s.42A, Criminal Justice and Policing Act 2001).

This chapter will consider the legal framework in these three statutory schemes governing harassment of an occupant of residential accommodation by someone who is that person's landlord or licensor or someone associated with such a person.

PROTECTION FROM EVICTION ACT 1977

No civil liability

One of the key problems identified in respect of s.1, PEA 1977 (considered in Chapter 3) is that the offences created do not give rise to a civil claim based on breach of statutory duty: see e.g. *McCall v Abelesz* [1976] QB 585, CA. In *McCall*, which concerned a claim brought solely pursuant to s.30(2) of the Rent Act 1965 (for these purposes, in broadly similar terms to what now appears in s.1, PEA 1977), the claimant brought proceedings in relation to a course of conduct which included the cutting off of utilities by the defendant landlord. The claimant obtained judgment at first instance, but the defendant appealed successfully to the Court of Appeal on the basis that s.30(2), RA 1965 provided for a criminal penalty only and did not give rise to a civil cause of action.

The Court of Appeal applied the approach of Atkin L.J. in *Phillips v Britannia Hygienic Laundry Co Ltd* [1923] 2 KB 832 at 840-84, where he stated:

> *"In my opinion, when an Act imposes a duty of commission or omission, the question whether a person aggrieved by a breach of the duty has a right of action depends on the intention of the Act. Was it intended to make the duty one which was owed to the party aggrieved as well as to the State, or was it a public duty only? That depends on the construction of the Act and the circumstances in which it was made and to which it relates. One question to be considered is, Does the Act contain reference to a remedy for breach of it? Prima facie if it does that is the only remedy. But that is not conclusive. The intention as disclosed by its scope and wording must still be regarded, and it may still be that, though the statute creates the duty and provides a penalty, the duty is nevertheless owed to individuals. Instances of this are Groves v. Lord Wimborne and Britannic Merthyr Coal Co. v. David. … [T]he question is whether these regulations, viewed in the circumstances in which they were made and to which they relate, were intended to impose a duty which is a public duty only or whether they were intended, in addition to the public duty, to impose a duty enforceable by an individual aggrieved…"*

In *McCall*, the Court of Appeal looked to the intention behind s.30, RA 1965 and reasoned, in the light of the above, that because s.30(4), RA 1965 preserved the existing civil remedies for harassment of a residential occupier (in the same way s.1(5), PEA 1977 does now), s.30(2), RA 1965 was clearly a penal provision and did not create a new statutory cause of action for damages. This lacuna was eventually filled to a limited extent by s.27, HA 1988.

Criminal offences

Harassment by any person (including a landlord) – s.1(3), PEA 1977

By s.1(3), PEA 1977:

> *"If any person with intent to cause the residential occupier of any premises—*
>
> > *(a) to give up the occupation of the premises or any part thereof; or*
> >
> > *(b) to refrain from exercising any right or pursuing any remedy in respect of the premises or part thereof;*
>
> *does acts likely to interfere with the peace or comfort of the residential occupier or members of his household, or persistently withdraws or withholds services reasonably required for the occupation of the premises as a residence, he shall be guilty of an offence."*

It is important to distinguish the actus reus and mens rea, both of which must be proved to establish the offence. As for the actus reus, the accused must have either:

- acted in a manner likely to interfere with the peace or comfort of a residential occupier or members of the occupier's household, or
- persistently withdrawn or withheld services reasonably required for residential occupation.

On the issue of mens rea, the defendant must have intended to cause the residential occupier either:

- to give up his or her occupation of the whole or part of the premises; or
- to refrain from exercising any right or pursuing any remedy in respect of the whole or part of the premises.

At common law, there is a rebuttable presumption of fact that a man intends the natural and probable consequences of his acts: *Frankland v R; Moore v R* [1987] A.C. 576; *R v Hyam* [1975] A.C. 55; *R v Moloney* [1985] A.C. 905; *R v Hancock* [1986] A.C. 455.

In *Schon v Camden LBC* (1986) 18 H.L.R. 341, QBD, a landlord asked his tenant to vacate her flat whilst refurbishment works were carried out to the flat above hers. She refused and those works resulted in a ceiling collapsing into her flat and rendering it uninhabitable. The Divisional Court, in allowing an appeal against conviction, held that, in the context of a case concerning only interference with peace or comfort under s.1(3)(a), s.1(3) does not constitute two different offences based on which of two intentions might apply; the act constituting the offence is an act calculated to interfere with the peace or comfort of the residential occupier; that act may be done with one of two intentions; to cause the residential occupier either to give up occupation of the premises or to refrain from exercising any right. Therefore, a local authority charging an accused under s.1(3), PEA 1977 should express the count on the indictment as one charge with alternative intentions (or make two alternative charges).

The Court in *Schon* also held that "occupation" was to be given the same meaning as in the Rent Acts and "give up" meant "give up permanently", distinguishing *Yuthiwattana*, above in the process.

If a person acts in a way which interferes with the peace or comfort of the residential occupier without either intention under s.1(3), PEA 1977 but, having acted in that manner, subsequently forms the intention and omits to put right his earlier interference in order to realise that intention, he will not be guilty of the offence in s.1(3): *Ahmad (Zafar)* (1987) 84 Cr. App. R. 64, CA.

Harassment by a landlord – s.1(3A), PEA 1977

> *"Subject to subsection (3B) below, the landlord of a residential occupier or an agent of the landlord shall be guilty of an offence if—*

> *(a) he does acts likely to interfere with the peace or comfort of the residential occupier or members of his household, or*
>
> *(b) he persistently withdraws or withholds services reasonably required for the occupation of the premises in question as a residence,*
>
> *and (in either case) he knows, or has reasonable cause to believe, that that conduct is likely to cause the residential occupier to give up the occupation of the whole or part of the premises or to refrain from exercising any right or pursuing any remedy in respect of the whole or part of the premises."*

This subsection was inserted by the Housing Act 1988, s.29. It relates specifically to landlords and their agents and removed the uncertainty of proving intent in s.1(3), PEA 1977.

Residential occupier

For these purposes, "residential occupier", in relation to any premises, means a person occupying the premises as a residence, whether under a contract or by virtue of any enactment or rule of law giving him the right to remain in occupation or restricting the right of any other person to recover possession of the premises.

In *R. v Blankley* [1979] Crim LR 166, the definition was held not to cover a licensee whose licence had expired. Despite such occupants being excluded from the protection of s.1, 1977 Act, s.6, Criminal Law Act 1977 provides that (subject to certain exceptions) any person who, without lawful authority, uses or threatens violence (against the person or property – s.6(4)) for the purpose of securing entry into any premises for himself or for any other person is guilty of an offence, provided that:

a) there is someone present on those premises at the time who is opposed to the entry which the violence is intended to secure; and

b) the person using or threatening the violence knows that that is the case.

It is important, therefore, to ensure that no positive acts occur which may be construed as contravening s.6, CLA 1977 even where a person has no entitlement to remain in occupation as a matter of law.

"Landlord"

"Landlord" for these purposes means the person who would be entitled to occupation of the premises, but for the residential occupier's right to remain in occupation of the premises, or a restriction on the person's right to recover possession of the premises. It also includes any superior landlord under whom that person derives title: s.1(3C), PEA 1977.

This designedly broad definition would include a licensor and any person from whom that licensor derives his title.

"Acts"

A single "act" is sufficient: Interpretation Act 1978 s.6(c); *R v Evangelos Polycarpou* [1978] 9 H.L.R. 129, CA.

An offence is not committed if the landlord fails to act: *R. v Ahmad* (1986) 18 H.L.R 416, CA.

The offence cannot be committed by the owner withholding or withdrawing something which he has been providing voluntarily: *McCall v Abelesz* [1976] QB 585. Query whether this is correct given the subsequent decision on *R v Burke* [1991] 1 AC 135, where the House of Lords held that interference with peace and comfort might arise from acts which did not constitute a breach of contract.

In *Mitchell* [1994] Crim.L.R. 66, CA, it was held that where several different acts were alleged in a single count contrary to s.1(3A), PEA 1977 each of which was enough to sustain a conviction, and there was a realistic risk that the jury might think they each could find a different act proved so long as they were unanimous that an act had taken place, they should be directed that they must be unanimous as to at least one particular act.

A prosecuting authority must ensure that that the count on the indictment under s.1(3A)(b), PEA 1977 includes reference to "persistently" as this is an element of the offence that must be proved: *R v Abrol* [1972] Crim LR 318 (a case decided in relation to the similarly worded provision in s.30(2), Rent Act 1965, referred to above).

Intention

In *McCall v Abelesz* [1976] QB 585, a case concerning s.30(2) of the Rent Act 1965, which was in identical terms to s.1(3), PEA 1977 prior to its amendment by the HA 1988 (changing "calculated" to "likely"), Ormrod L.J. said, at p. 597:

> *"Subsection (2) is even more clearly a penal provision. First, a specific intent or mens rea must be proved before the offence is complete; that is, the intent to cause the residential occupier either to give up the premises or to refrain from exercising some right in respect of the premises. Secondly, the actus reus of the subsection is the doing of acts calculated to interfere with the peace or comfort of the occupier or the persistent withholding or withdrawal of services reasonably required for the occupation of the premises."*

It appears that the necessary mental element of the offence has changed in the light of the HA 1988 amendments because the prosecution need not prove beyond reasonable doubt that the acts were "calculated" to interfere with the occupant's peace or comfort but merely that they were the "likely" consequence of those acts.

Prosecuting authorities

Proceedings for an offence under the PEA 1977 may be instituted by councils of districts and London boroughs; councils of Welsh counties and county boroughs; the Common Council of the City of London; and the Council of the Isles of Scilly: s.6, PEA 1977.

Most local authorities will have specific processes in place pursuant to which they prosecute this (and other related) offences. The starting point for claimants wishing to instigate criminal proceedings against a perpetrator is to approach the local authority for the area in which the premises are located to report the offence.

Penalty

A person guilty of an offence under s.1(3A), PEA 1977 is liable:

a) on summary conviction, to a fine not exceeding the prescribed sum or to imprisonment for a term not exceeding 6 months or to both;

b) on conviction on indictment, to a fine or to imprisonment for a term not exceeding 2 years or to both: s.1(4), PEA 1977.

As with contraventions of s.1(1), PEA 1977, the offence is triable either way and therefore the six-month time-limit for laying a complaint to the Magistrates' Court does not apply.

Scope of the offences

It is not necessary for an act by the defendant to be an actionable civil wrong in order to constitute an offence under s.1(3), PEA 1977: *R. v Burke (Alisdair David)* [1991] 1 AC 135; (1990) 22 HLR 433 (approving *R. v Yuthiwattana (Helen)* (1985) 80 Cr App R 55; (1984) 16 HLR 49).

Vicarious liability

A person cannot be guilty of an offence under s.1(3A), PEA 1977, on the basis that he is vicariously liable for another person's actions; a landlord may be found guilty of an offence under s.1(3A), PEA 1977 if he aids, abets, counsels or procures his agent to commit criminal acts or if the agent acted in conspiracy with the landlord: *R. v Quereshi* [2011] EWCA Crim 1584; [2011] HLR 34. In *Gibson v Douglas* [2016] EWCA Civ 1266, the eviction was carried out by the police, not the defendant, who was found not to be responsible for the actions of the police.

No prejudice to civil claim

As set out above, nothing in s.1, PEA 1977 prejudices any liability or remedy in civil proceedings: s.1(5), PEA 1977.

Offence by a company

Where an offence under s.1, PEA 1977 is committed by a body corporate is proved to have been committed with the consent or connivance of, or to be attributable to any neglect on the part of, any director, manager or secretary or other similar officer of the body corporate or any person who was purporting to act in any such capacity, he as well as the body corporate is guilty of that offence: s.1(6), PEA 1977.

Defences

There is a defence where:

a) the person does not know, nor has reasonable cause to believe, that that conduct is likely to cause the residential occupier to give up the occupation of the whole or part of the premises or to refrain from exercising any right or pursuing any remedy in respect of the whole or part of the premises: s.1(3A), PEA 1977; or

b) if he proves that he had reasonable grounds for doing the acts or withdrawing or withholding the services in question: s.1(3B), PEA 1977. This creates a legal burden on the accused to establish the reasonableness of his grounds for withdrawing or withholding services: *Att.-Gen.'s Ref (No. 1 of 2004),* above.

The inclusion of a statutory defence to s.1(3A), PEA 1977 reflects (i) the broader set of circumstances in which the offence arises compared to s.1(3), PEA 1977, and (ii) the change in the mental element of the offence (such that the prosecution no longer needs to prove *an intent to cause* the residential occupier to give up the accommodation; it is sufficient to prove knowledge or reasonable cause to believe that this would be the likely outcome).

Breach of contract

In the same way that a tenant who is unlawfully evicted from their residential accommodation would be able to sue for breach of the express or implied covenant for quiet enjoyment, a person who is subjected to harassment falling short of eviction would be able to sue.

As previously set out in Chapter 2, the types of acts which breach the covenant for quiet enjoyment would cover include attempts to drive out a tenant from possession of the premises through targeted persecution and intimidation (including threats to evict without due process and remove a tenant's personal possessions): *Kenny v Preen* [1963] 1 QB 499; *Sampson v Floyd* [1989] 2 EGLR 49, and cutting off utilities: *Perera v Vandiyar* [1953] 1 WLR 672.

PROTECTION FROM HARASSMENT ACT 1997

Meaning of "harassment"

"Harassment" is not defined in the PHA 1997 save insofar as it includes alarming a person and/or causing them distress: s.7(2), PHA 1997. It has been held to comprise conduct which is oppressive, unreasonable or unacceptable and the gravity of which would sustain criminal liability: *Majrowseki v Guy's and St Thomas's NHS Trust* [2006] UKHL 34; [2007] 1 AC 224.

In this context, in *Hourani v Thomson* [2017] EWHC 432 (QB), Warby J summarised the applicable principles:

> *"[138] … s.7(2) of the 1997 Act, which provides that 'references to harassing a person include alarming the person or causing the person distress'. This is not a definition of the tort. It is merely guidance as to one element of it. Nor is it an exhaustive statement of the consequences that harassment may involve.*

The Supreme Court gave further guidance in Hayes v Willoughby [2013] UKSC 17 [2013] 1 WLR 935, where Lord Sumption SC said at [1] that harassment is '... an ordinary English word with a well understood meaning. Harassment is a persistent and deliberate course of unreasonable and oppressive conduct, targeted at another person, which is calculated to and does cause that person alarm, fear or distress.'

[139] As these words suggest, behaviour must reach a certain level of seriousness before it amounts to harassment within the scope of PHA s.1. That is not least because the 1997 Act creates both a tort and, by s.2, a crime of harassment. The authoritative exposition of this point is that of Lord Nicholls in Majrowski v Guy's and St Thomas's NHS Trust [2007] 1 AC 224 [30]:

> *'[Where] the quality of the conduct said to constitute harassment is being examined, courts will have in mind that irritations, annoyances, even a measure of upset, arise at times in everybody's day-to-day dealings with other people. Courts are well able to recognise the boundary between conduct which is unattractive, even unreasonable, and conduct which is oppressive and unacceptable. To cross the boundary from the regrettable to the unacceptable the gravity of the misconduct must be of an order which would sustain criminal liability under section 2.'*

[140] There must, therefore, be conduct on at least two occasions which is, from an objective standpoint, calculated to cause alarm or distress and oppressive, and unacceptable to such a degree that it would sustain criminal liability: see Dowson v Chief Constable of Northumbria Police [2010] EWHC 2612 (QB) [142] (Simon J)."

The aforementioned paragraphs were cited with approval recently in *Oliver v Javad Shaikh* [2019] EWHC 3389 (QB) *per* Knowles J (at [81]).

By way of example, in *APW v WPA* [2012] EWHC 3151 (QB) at [43], Tugendhat J noted that sending distressing text messages was arguably a course of conduct amounting to harassment within the PHA 1997. The facts of that case largely influenced the decision and so it is not inevitably the case that the sending of text messages would amount to harassment, it will turn on the specific circumstances.

The prohibition

Harassment of individuals

By s.1(1), PHA 1997, a person must not pursue a course of conduct which amounts to harassment of another, and which he knows or ought to know amounts to harassment of the other.

Harassment of more than one person

By s.1(1A), PHA 1997, a person must not pursue a course of conduct

a) which involves harassment of two or more persons, and

b) which he knows or ought to know involves harassment of those persons, and

c) by which he intends to persuade any person (whether or not one of those mentioned above)

    i. not to do something that he is entitled or required to do, or

    ii. to do something that he is not under any obligation to do.

Section 1(1A), PHA 1997 along with other related provisions considered below was inserted by s.125 of the Serious Organised Crime and Police Act 2005. The purpose appears to be to prevent harassment of persons such that they or any third parties are persuaded to act (or not act) in a particular way. The mischief this was primarily intended to address was acts of protest against animal testing (and particularly those cases where professionals and their families lived in close proximity to the laboratories in which they worked).

The victim(s)

References to a person, in the context of the harassment of a person, are references to a person who is an individual: s.7(5), PHA 1997.

Course of conduct

Conduct includes speech: s.7(4), PHA 1997. A 'course of conduct' must involve, in the case of conduct in relation to a single person, conduct on at least two occasions in relation to that person: s.7(3)(a), PHA 1997 and, in the case of conduct in relation to two or more persons, conduct on at least one occasion in relation to each of those persons: s.7(3)(b), PHA 1997. It is not enough for there to be two separate and individual incidents without cogent linking conduct between them: *R v Hills* [2001] 1 FLR 580. The fewer the incidents and the more time between them, the less likely it is that the court will find they constitute a "course of conduct": *Lau v DPP* [2000] 1 FLR 799.

By s.1(2), PHA 1997, the person whose course of conduct is in question ought to know that it amounts to or involves harassment of another if a reasonable person in possession of the same information would think the course of conduct amounted to or involved harassment of the other. The test is wholly objective: *DPP v H* [1997] 1 WLR 1406.

Counselling, procuring, aiding and abetting

By s.7(3A), PHA 1977, a person's conduct on any occasion is taken, if aided, abetted, counselled or procured by another:

a) to be conduct on that occasion of the other (as well as conduct of the person whose conduct it is); and

b) to be conduct in relation to which the other's knowledge and purpose, and what he ought to have known, are the same as they were in relation to what was contemplated or reasonably foreseeable at the time of the aiding, abetting, counselling or procuring.

Intended target

In *Levi v Bates* [2015] EWCA Civ 206, B had publicised L's home address and telephone number as a result of which people both attended at his address and made threatening telephone calls to the house. This caused distress to his wife. The Court of Appeal held that there was no requirement that a claimant be the intended target of the harassment, only that he be a foreseeable victim of it.

Criminal offences

Under s.2, PHA 1997, if a person pursues a course of conduct which amounts to harassment under s.1, he is guilty of an offence and liable - on summary conviction only – to imprisonment for a term not exceeding six months, or a fine not exceeding level 5 on the standard scale, or both.

Defence

A defendant has a defence if s/he shows on the balance of probabilities that:

a) the course of conduct was pursued for the purpose of preventing or detecting crime;

b) it was pursued under any enactment or rule of law or to comply with any condition or requirement imposed by any person under any enactment, and/or

c) in the particular circumstances the pursuit of the course of conduct was reasonable: s.1(3), PHA 1997.

It is insufficient for a defendant to merely assert that the course of conduct was pursued for the purpose of preventing or detecting crime; he must demonstrate that he pursued the course of conduct as a rational response to a rational consideration of whether there was criminality: *Hayes v Willoughby* [2013] UKSC 17; [2013] 1 W.L.R. 935. The Court went on to find (at [17], [21]) that, "[t]he proposition that the purpose specified in [s.]1(3)(a) must be the sole purpose of the alleged harasser is indefensible. A person's purposes are almost always to some extent mixed, and the ordinary principle is that the relevant purpose is the dominant one."

That the course of conduct is caused by mental illness is not a defence: *R v Colohan (Sean Peter)* [2001] EWCA Crim 1251.

Furthermore, conduct in breach of an injunction which has been properly served and where the contemnors have full notice its terms cannot be reasonable in the absence of a wholly exceptional excuse such as breaching a prohibition to enter land to rescue someone: *DPP v Moseley (Joanna)* Times, June 23, 1999 (QBD) (*per* Roch L.J.).

Restraining orders

In addition to the power to make an injunction, a court sentencing or otherwise dealing with a person convicted of an offence may (in addition) make a restraining order, on conviction (pursuant to s.5, PHA 1997) or on acquittal (pursuant to s.5A, PHA 1997), where it considers it necessary to do so to protect a person from harassment by the defendant. Breach of either of which is an offence.

Other offences of relevance

There is another offence contained within the PHA 1997 which may have relevance to a claim for harassment in the context of a landlord and tenant relationship, namely "putting people in fear of violence": s.4, PHA 1997.

Civil claims and injunctions

Section 3(1), PHA 1997 provides that any actual or apprehended breach of s.1(1), PHA 1997 may be the subject of a civil claim by anyone who is or may be the victim of the course of conduct. On such a claim, damages may be awarded for (among other things) any anxiety caused by the harassment and any financial loss resulting from the harassment: s.3(2), PHA 1997.

Practitioners should note the use of the phrase "actual or apprehended" in s.3(1), PHA 1997. It is not necessary, for the purposes of obtaining an injunction to prevent harassment to show a course of conduct already exists which will continue unless restrained. This begs the question what circumstances would be sufficient to show that an "apprehended" breach of s.1(1), PHA 1997 was enough to merit the court exercising its discretion to make an injunction. The reference to "apprehended" creates a statutory footing for what is commonly known as a *quia timet* injunction (granted where no wrong has been done although it is threatened). In cases involving nuisance, the courts' approach is that "[s]uch an injunction should not, ordinarily, be granted unless the plaintiff can show a strong probability that, unless restrained, the defendant will do something which will cause the plaintiff irreparable harm – that is to say, harm which, if it occurs, cannot be reversed or restrained by an immediate interlocutory injunction and cannot be adequately compensated by an award for damages": *Lloyd v Symonds* [1998] EWCA Civ 511; applied in *Islington LBC v Elliott* [2012] EWCA Civ 56.

It plainly will be much easier to do so in a case where a course of conduct can be established but, in cases of accommodation-related harassment, the first instance of conduct designed to force the occupant to leave the premises may be followed up by the landlord changing the locks.

In such cases, it will be necessary for the occupant to provide detailed instructions on any conversations or exchange of emails/text messages with the landlord demonstrating a propensity toward removing the occupant without taking lawful steps. A defective s.21 notice (where the tenant raised a failure to licence a HMO or comply with gas safety requirements) coupled with messages saying the landlord wanted the tenant to leave and followed up by the cutting off of utilities is far more likely to persuade a court that there is a legitimate basis for the apprehension of further conduct which would amount to harassment than e.g. asserting without more that the utilities had been cut off (for which a landlord might have a plausible explanation).

In *Burris v Azadani* [1995] 1 W.L.R. 1372, the Court of Appeal held that injunctions under s.3A, PHA 1997 could be granted to restrain conduct which was not in and of itself unlawful. In that case, this included cycling past the claimant's property.

In assessing whether harassment is established objectively, regard must be had to the impact of the conduct on the rights of any children in determining whether a person ought to have known that his conduct amounts to harassment and to whether the s.1(3)(c) defence (discussed below) is made out: see *Othman v English National Resistance* [2013] EWHC 1421 (QB). This may be of particular relevance if a landlord is acting in a way which intimidates children in occupation of the property, or which interferes with their ability to enjoy the premises (such as not wanting to go out in the garden).

Where the High Court or the county court grants an injunction for the purpose of restraining the defendant from pursuing any conduct which amounts to harassment, and that injunction is breached, the claimant may apply for the issue of a warrant for the arrest of the defendant: s.3(3).

Injunctions involving harassment of more than one person

Section 3A(1), PHA 1997 enables a person to apply to the County Court or High Court for an injunction to prevent an actual or apprehended breach of s.1(1A), PHA 1997, by any person. By s.3A(2), PHA 1977, in such a case, not only can the victim of the harassment apply for an injunction but so can any third party who is the intended target of the persuasion.

Procedure

In the absence of a claim for other relief such as damages and reinstatement for unlawful eviction (in which case the normal Part 7 procedure discussed in Chapter 10 will apply), any claim for harassment under the PHA 1997 must be commenced using Claim Form N208 and follow the CPR Part 8 procedure.

The claim must be commenced in the Queen's Bench Division if issued in the High Court, or at a hearing centre in the County Court which serves the address for service (residential or commercial) of either the claimant or defendant (r.65.28).

Consistently with the CPR Part 8 procedure, the following procedural requirements must be followed:

- The claim form must state:

  (i) that Part 8 applies;

  (ii) the question which the claimant wants the court to decide; or the remedy which the claimant is seeking and the legal basis for the claim to that remedy; and

  (iii) that the claim is being made under s.3, PHA 1997: CPR r.8.2.

- Evidence can be provided by witness statement of affidavit but the claimant may also rely on the contents of the claim form provided that it has been verified by a statement of truth: CPR r.8.5(7) and PD 8A, para.7.2.

- The claimant must file any written evidence (whether by witness statement or affidavit) on which he intends to rely when he files his claim form. He must serve the claim form and written evidence together: CPR r.8.5(1) and (2).

- The defendant must file an acknowledgment of service within 14 days of service of the claim form: CPR r.8.3(a). The acknowledgement must state whether the defendant intends to contest the claim and if he seeks a remedy different from that in the claim form, what that remedy is: CPR r.8.3(2). If the defendant fails to file the acknowledgement of service in time he is prevented from taking part in the hearing unless the court grants permission: CPR r.8.4(2).

- If the defendant wishes to rely on evidence, he must file it with the acknowledgment of service: CPR r.8.5(3), and serve a copy of it on the other parties: CPR r.8.5(4).
- Where the defendant has included written evidence, the claimant has a further 14 days in which to file and serve evidence in reply: CPR r.8.5(5).
- If written evidence is served out of time or either party wants to rely on additional evidence, the court's permission on application is required: CPR r.8.6(1)(b) and PD 8A 7.4. The court may require or permit evidence to be given orally at the hearing: CPR r.8.6(2).

Part 8 applies where there is no substantial dispute of fact. If the defendant considers there is such a dispute, and the Part 8 procedure is inappropriate to determine it, he should say so when he files the acknowledgment of service and give reasons: CPR r.8.8. This is likely to result in the claim being reallocated to Part 7 at the first hearing.

Applications for an injunction should be made in the claim form: CPR r.8.2. The general procedure for making an application for interim relief is considered further in Chapter 7.

Limitation periods for damages claims

As with any claim in tort, the limitation period for bringing a claim for damages under s.3, PHA 1997 is 6 years.

Section 11(1A), Limitation Act 1980 (special time limit for actions in respect of personal injuries) provides that the three-year longstop for bringing proceedings for personal injury does not apply to any action brought for damages under s.3, PHA 1997.

Enforcement in cases of breach of the injunction

As with any tort, an application for an injunction can be brought to restrain it. There is no specific procedure governing applications for injunctions restraining harassment and CPR Part 25 and PD 25A therefore applies (see Chapter 7).

Breach of the injunction can be enforced by committal proceedings (see Chapter 8) or as a criminal offence (note, these two enforcement methods are mutually exclusive: s.3(7) and (8) PHA 1997).

Warrant of arrest

Where the breach is dealt with via committal proceedings, it is noteworthy that there is no provision for a power of arrest (as is the case e.g. in anti-social behaviour proceedings). A warrant of arrest must be sought from the court which granted the injunction – whether the High Court or County Court: s.3(3) and (4), PHA 1997.

The application must be substantiated on oath and the court must be satisfied that there are reasonable grounds for believing the defendant is in breach: s.3(5), PHA 1997. By CPR r.65.29, it must also be made in accordance with Part 23, may be made without notice, the affidavit in support must set out the grounds for the application; state whether the claimant has informed the police of the conduct of the defendant as described in the affidavit; and state whether, to the claimant's knowledge, criminal proceedings are being pursued.

On arrest, the judge before whom a person is brought following his arrest (which cannot be a district judge as the statute does not provide for such) may deal with the matter; or adjourn the proceedings. Where the proceedings are adjourned and the arrested person is released (there is no power to bail) the matter must be dealt with (whether by the same or another judge) within 28 days of the date on which the arrested person appears in court; and the arrested person must be given not less than 2 days' notice of the hearing: CPR r.65.30. An application for the defendant's committal could be brought under CPR Part 81 which would negate the time constraints imposed in respect of the warrant of arrest.

Criminal offence

Breach of an injunction granted by the High Court or County Court under s.3, PHA 1997 is also a criminal offence: s.3(6), PHA 1997, punishable, on conviction on indictment, to imprisonment for a term not exceeding five years, or a fine, or both, or, on summary conviction, to imprisonment for a term not exceeding six months, or a fine not exceeding the statutory maximum, or both.

CRIMINAL JUSTICE AND POLICE ACT 2001

Section 42A(1) and (3), CJPA 2001 provide that a person commits an offence if:

a) that person (whether alone or not) is present outside or in the vicinity of any premises that are used by any individual ("the resident") as his dwelling;

b) that person is present there for the purpose (by his presence or otherwise) of representing to the resident or another individual (whether or not one who uses the premises as his dwelling), or of persuading the resident or such another individual

    i. that he should not do something that he is entitled or required to do; or

    ii. that he should do something that he is not under any obligation to do;

c) that person

    i. intends his presence to amount to the harassment of, or to cause alarm or distress to, the resident; or

    ii. knows or ought to know that his presence is likely to result in the harassment of, or to cause alarm or distress to, the resident; and

d) the presence of that person

   i. amounts to the harassment of, or causes alarm or distress to, any person falling within s.42A(2); or

   ii. is likely to result in the harassment of, or to cause alarm or distress to, any such person.

"Dwelling" for these purposes means any structure or part of a structure occupied as a person's home or as other living accommodation (whether the occupation is separate or shared with others) but does not include any part not so occupied, and for this purpose *"structure"* includes a tent, caravan, vehicle, vessel or other temporary or movable structure (s.8, POA 1986): s.42A(7), CJPA 2001.

This offence catches harassment of any person if he is a resident or a person in that resident's dwelling or any person in another dwelling in the vicinity of the resident's dwelling: s.42A(2), CJPA 2001. The offence would cover harassment of homeowners as well as tenants or licensees.

Whether a person "ought to know that his presence is likely to result in the harassment of, or to cause alarm or distress to, the resident" for the purposes of s.42A(1)(c)(ii), CJPA 2001 is assessed objectively: s.42A(4), CJPA 2001.

If convicted of the offence under s.42A, CJPA 2001, a person is liable, on summary conviction, to imprisonment for a term (currently) not exceeding six months or to a fine not exceeding level 4 on the standard scale, or to both.

POINTS TO NOTE

- **A claim for unlawful eviction does not automatically include a remedy for harassing behaviour. The conduct may constitute a breach of the covenant for quiet enjoyment but that will depend broadly on whether the person was a tenant and/or** the nature and extent of the harassment. It is important to ensure a separate claim is made for harassment within the claim for unlawful eviction (using the procedure under CPR Part 7). This will enable not only damages to reflect that additional suffering but an application for an injunction to restrain future, similar conduct (which will be particularly important if legal proceedings are ongoing and there is a concern about retaliatory acts or witness interference).

- If a separate or freestanding claim for harassment is brought, it must follow the CPR Part 8 procedure.

- Prosecuting a person for harassment will not necessarily provide the victim with any protection or reassurance and certainly will not result in comparable financial compensation for the distress caused. As such, civil proceedings are likely to be the preferable option in the first instance.

- The speed with which relief can be sought weighs heavily in favour of applying for injunctions under s.3, PHA 1997 (following the procedure in CPR Part 25 and PD 25A, considered in Chapter 7) and, in the event of any breach, enforcing them through committal proceedings in the county court (following the procedure in CPR Part 81, considered in Chapter 8).

CHAPTER SIX
DAMAGES

This chapter considers how damages are assessed in civil claims for unlawful eviction and harassment. Again, there is a clear distinction between claims for breach of contract and claims in tort (including any entitlement to statutory damages pursuant to s.28, HA 1988).

In order to maximise the potential damages available to a claimant, both contractual and tortious causes of action should be pleaded, most commonly, breach of the covenant for quiet enjoyment alongside a claim for breach of s.3, PEA 1977 or s.27, HA 1988 where appropriate and/or trespass. This chapter will therefore look at how damages are calculated for breach of contract first, followed by tort and thereafter the specific approach adopted in unlawful eviction and harassment claims.

CONTRACT

Contractual damages compensate a claimant for damage, loss or injury suffered as a result of a breach of contract: *Johnson v Agnew* [1980] AC 367, 400. The approach to assessing that loss starts with considering how the claimant can (in monetary terms) be placed in the same position as if the contract had been performed: *Robinson v Harman* 154 ER 363; *Golden Strait Corp v Nippon Yusen Kubishika Kaisha* [2007] UKHL 12, [2007] 2 AC 353.

Causation

As contractual damages are designed to compensate for loss caused by the breach, it is necessary to assess the position of the claimant as a result of the breach and the position he would have been in but for the breach. The aim of the damages award is to put the claimant into the position he would have been in if the breach of contract had not occurred. For that reason, the loss is often referred to as "expectation damages".

In order to recover damages for breach of contract, the claimant must show that the breach of contract was the "effective" or "dominant" cause of the loss. This is largely a matter of common sense for the trial judge: *Galoo v Bright Grahame Murray* [1994] 1 WLR 1360, 1374–1375.

Limitations on recovery

The recovery of damages for breach of contract is limited in three respects by the principles of: mitigation, remoteness and assumption of responsibility.

Mitigation

A claimant cannot recover for losses which he could have avoided by taking reasonable steps or did avoid by taking reasonable (or more than reasonable) steps but he can recover the expense incurred in taking the step: see *Thai Airways International Public Co Ltd v KI Holdings Co Ltd* [2015] EWHC 1250 (Comm) (at [31]-[38]) for a detailed consideration of the principles.

Remoteness

The claimant will recover for losses only if they arose "in the usual course of things" or were losses that were contemplated by the parties at the time the contract was made: *Hadley v Baxendale* (1854) 9 Ex 341; *Victoria Laundry (Windsor) Ltd v Newman Industries Ltd* [1949] 2 KB 528; *Koufos v C Czarnikow Ltd (The Heron II)* [1969] 1 AC 350.

Assumption of responsibility

A claimant will not recover losses that arose even in the usual course of things if the defendant could not reasonably be regarded as assuming responsibility for losses of the particular kind suffered: *Transfield*

Shipping Inc v Mercator Shipping Inc (The Achilleas) [2008] UKHL 48; [2009] 1 AC 61.

TORT

Damages in tort

Contrary to the position in contract, damages in tort are awarded to put the party against whom the tort was committed back into the position he would have been in had it not taken place: *James Livingstone v The Rawyards Coal Company (Limited)* (1879) 6 R 922.

Causation

If the cause of action relied on is harassment under the PHA 1997 or dishonest trespass to goods (i.e. where the landlord knows the goods are not his) then all losses caused directly by the tort are recoverable: *Jones v Ruth* [2011] EWCA Civ 804, [2012] 1 All ER 490; *Kuwait Airways Corp v Iraqi Airways Co* [2002] UKHL 19. For the other causes of action considered in this book, the claimant has to show that his losses were a reasonably foreseeable consequence of the tort.

In a claim for unlawful eviction with no element of harassment or trespass to goods therefore, the losses will be restricted to those which were reasonably foreseeable.

TYPES OF DAMAGE

In cases involving unlawful eviction and harassment, there are five potential types of damages available to a claimant: special damages, general damages, aggravated damages, exemplary damages and (where applicable) nominal damages.

Special damage

Special damages are those damages which can easily be quantified in monetary terms. In a claim for unlawful eviction, this is likely to include the cost of alternative accommodation, the difference between the cost of food which could be cooked at home and eating in restaurants or buying takeaways, and goods which have been destroyed or lost.

In a claim for harassment where e.g. the gas has been cut off it would be the increased cost of heating the property using electricity.

Where there has been conversion of the occupants' belongings, the market value of those belongings at the date of the conversion would be recoverable: see McGregor on Damages 20th Ed. at 38-006.

It is important therefore for advisors not to inadvertently seek to over-compensate a claimant by claiming (or not defending) special damages claims which seek to recover all sums resulting from the tort. Examples would include claiming all the accommodation costs incurred by an unlawful eviction without setting off what would have been the ongoing obligation for rent or occupation charge for so long as the occupant would have remained, or the full cost of eating out when the claimant would have paid for food to cook, or the cost of heating/lighting the property without setting off the cost that would have been incurred in any event for such utilities.

General damage

General damages are those losses which cannot easily be quantified in monetary terms such as damages for pain and suffering, harm, shock, distress, inconvenience, and physical injury. These are particularly relevant to claims for unlawful eviction and harassment where, leaving aside any damage to goods which may have been caused and the cost of any alternative accommodation, the main loss will be the distress of the eviction and subsequent lack of accommodation.

Uplift

From 1 April 2013, any assessment of general damages claims for unlawful eviction and harassment involve an uplift to the sum by 10%: *Simmons v Castle* [2012] EWCA Civ 1288; [2013] CP Rep 3. This uplift reflects the changes to CFA funding arrangements and introduction of DBAs discussed in Chapter 9.

Generally only available in tort

These damages cannot be awarded for breach of contract unless the purpose of the contract was to provide pleasure, peace of mind, relaxation or freedom from molestation which the covenant for quiet enjoyment does not do: *Branchett v Beaney* (1992) 24 HLR 348, CA. In order to claim general damages, therefore, it is imperative that advisors plead a cause of action in tort such as trespass, harassment or nuisance.

Damages for trespass

In most cases involving unlawful eviction, the claimant will rely on trespass as a cause of action in tort. The basis on which damages are assessed for trespass to land is complex owing to the various different types of trespass to land that can occur (e.g. placing advertising, carrying out business on land, eviction etc.). The normal measure is that described above, namely that damages for tort are compensatory and assessed by looking at the position the claimant would have been in *but for* the tort, however, damages can be awarded to reflect the benefit to the trespasser of his unlawful use of the land: see *Attorney General v Blake* [2001] 1 A.C. 268 HL per Lord Nicholls at 278E–G (e.g. the profit obtained from the trespass in *Stadium Capital Holdings v St Marylebone Properties Co Plc* [2010] EWCA Civ 952) or by determining the hypothetical negotiations which would have taken place, such as the value of the licence fee that ought to have been obtained in *Bocardo SA v Star Energy UK Onshore Ltd* [2010] UKSC 35; [2011] 1 AC 380.

In unlawful eviction cases, the basis on which damages for trespass are calculated is unclear to say the least. At first blush the process seems straightforward: but for the unlawful nature of the eviction or the harassing conduct, what would the position have been and what losses have been incurred as a result? However, it is impossible to glean from the authorities any uniform approach and rather, guidance has been taken from the amounts awarded in previous cases. This issue was considered by the Court of Appeal in *Smith v Khan* [2018] EWCA Civ 1137; [2018] H.L.R. 31 (see below) and whilst providing some degree of clarity on the likely measure of damages for being out of possession as a result of a trespass (calculated by way of a daily rate), the decision has done little to explain how that measure is reached on traditional contract/tort principles.

Damages for harassment

By s.3(2), PHA 1997 damages for harassment include damages for any anxiety caused by the harassment and any resulting financial loss.

In *Jones v Ruth*, a case concerning a neighbour dispute where psychiatric injury to one party had resulted in a loss of earnings for several years, the Court of Appeal overturned the trial judge's refusal to award damages for this head of loss (on the basis that damages for personal injury do not arise out of nuisance and such losses were not reasonably foreseeable in relation to the claim for harassment), reasoning that s.3(2), PHA 1997 did not require that such losses be reasonably foreseeable.

In *Martins v Choudhary* [2007] EWCA Civ 1379; [2008] 1 W.L.R. 617, a claim for harassment concerning racist remarks and a vehicle collision, the Court of Appeal endorsed the bands-based approach to assessing quantum for injury to feelings short of psychiatric injury in *Vento v Chief Constable of West Yorkshire* [2002] EWCA Civ 1871, [2003] I.C.R. 318. That this was the proper approach in all cases was doubted in *S & D Property Investments Ltd v Nisbet* where consideration was given to the "modest" amounts in damages likely to be awarded under the PHA 1997 and the focus in *Vento* on discrimination which necessarily involves an element of humiliation.

In *Barkhuysen v Hamilton* [2016] EWHC 2858 (QB); [2018] 2 W.L.R. 9 Warby J gave a succinct summary of the approach to assessing quantum for injury to feelings (including anxiety) not amounting to psychiatric harm (at [160]):

"Guidelines for damages in harassment were given by the Court of Appeal in Vento [...] The court identified three broad bands for compensation for injured feelings: a top band for very serious cases, a middle band for moderately serious cases and a third band for less serious cases, such as isolated or one-off occurrences. Only in the most exceptional cases, it was said, would it be appropriate to award more than the top band and awards of less than £500 were to be avoided as they risked appearing derisory. Again, adjustment for inflation is required. The former adjustment was made by the Employment Appeal Tribunal in 2009 in Da'Bell v National Society for the Prevention of Cruelty to Children [2010] IRLR 19. Inflation since then has been some 20%, leading to a range in band 3 of up to £7,200, a middle band from £7,200 to £21,600 and a top band from £21,600 to £36,000. A Simmons v Castle adjustment is also required."

Since then, on 5.9.17, the Presidents of the Tribunals in England & Wales issued Presidential Guidance which applied to claims for damages for injury to feelings presented on or after 11.9.17. That Guidance was updated on 23.3.18, 25.3.19 and most recently on 6.4.20. The revised bands in the Guidance are now as follows:

- **£900** to **£9,000** for less serious cases, such as where an act of discrimination is an isolated occurrence.

- **£9,000** to **£27,000** for serious cases which do not merit an award in the highest band

- **£27,000** to **£45,000** for the most serious cases, such as where there has been a lengthy campaign of discriminatory harassment on the ground of sex or race. The most exceptional of cases may merit a higher award.

The bands take account of the 10% *Simmons* uplift referred to above.

Whether a case falls within the less serious, serious or very serious "*Vento*" bands will turn on the facts but a "typical" case of unlawful eviction with associated harassment (involving threatening texts, attending the property unannounced and issuing demands for rent or threats of eviction, turning off utilities and other conduct calculated to drive the tenant out of the property) tends to fall towards the top end of the "less serious" category or bottom end of the "serious" category.

By way of example, in *Kaye v Lees*, Central London County Court, 2 January 2019, HHJ Roberts awarded damages of £12,000 for distress caused by a neighbour's harassment, which ultimately led to the claimant moving out of his home and selling it. In so doing the court considered both the *Vento* guidelines and looked at the matter more broadly. The court also compensated the claimant for his financial losses (including diminution in value of the property as a result of the claimant's actions) of nearly £85,000. No aggravated damages were awarded.

Aggravated damages

As the name implies, aggravated damages compensate for aggravation to the claimant and for injury to his feelings of dignity and pride: *Drane v Evangelou* [1978] 1 W.L.R. 455. In that case, the sum of £1,000 was awarded for aggravation caused by the eviction. Aggravated damages may also be awarded in cases of trespass where the defendant's conduct has been high-handed, insulting or oppressive: see *Horsford v Bird* [2006] UKPC 3.

Aggravated damages are only available where the claim includes a cause of action in tort and, even then, on the established authorities, it must be a claim for trespass to land, assault or deceit. Most claims for unlawful eviction will plead trespass to land in the alternative to breach of covenant.

Examples of the types of "aggravation" which would likely feature in a claim for unlawful eviction would be:

- The embarrassment caused by the eviction (which would be further aggravated if done in public view);

- An eviction at night when it would be much more difficult to source alternative accommodation at short notice;
- Assault in the course of the eviction (including e.g. being dragged out the premises);
- An eviction involving children;
- The landlord having cleared out personal items such as underwear, photos etc.

In order to maximise the amount of aggravated damages recoverable by a claimant, the pleadings should include reference to the circumstances upon which this aspect of the claim relies.

Exemplary damages

The purpose of exemplary damages is to punish the tortfeasor and to deter him from similar behaviour in the future. These can only be claimed where:

a) they are expressly provided for by statute;

b) there has been oppressive conduct by servants of the Government; or,

c) the defendant's conduct has been calculated to make a profit which may well exceed the compensation available to the claimant: *Rookes v Barnard* [1964] AC 1129.

The third limb will be relevant to a claim for unlawful eviction and/or harassment. In *Cassell & Co Ltd v Broome* [1972] AC 1027, HL, it was held that it was unnecessary to identify a specific financial advantage that the landlord sought to gain, merely that the landlord sought to gain the premises in circumstances where either he could not obtain it at all or could only do so at a price greater than he was willing to pay. This would include evicting someone in order to avoid the expense of taking court proceedings.

In *Axa Insurance UK Plc v Financial Claims Solutions Ltd* [2018] EWCA Civ 1330; [2019] R.T.R. 1, Flaux LJ provided some important guidance on the approach to awarding exemplary damages, namely that it requires the Court to analyse the position *prospectively* when the tort is committed, at which time the tortfeasor may or may not ultimately achieve the profit it seeks to achieve (at [27]). It would be wrong, therefore, when determining whether to make an award to look at whether a profit has in fact been realised. Furthermore, the fact that compensation may be recovered by the claimant such as to disgorge the tortfeasor's profit does not bar an award of exemplary damages (at [28]), and it is irrelevant that criminal or contempt proceedings have been or could be brought (at [33]-[34]).

The pleadings must detail the basis upon which exemplary damages are claimed.

Nominal damages

Nominal damages are awarded to reflect wrongdoing against a person but where no financial or other loss has been caused. It is commonly awarded in relation to the tort of trespass where no loss or damage is caused.

Housing Act 1988, s.28 damages

In addition to the above, there is a specific statutory method for calculating damages for breach of s.27, HA 1988 which is contained in s.28 and states:

> *"(1) The basis for the assessment of damages referred to in section 27(3) above is the difference in value, determined as at the time immediately before the residential occupier ceased to occupy the premises in question as his residence, between—*
>
> > *(a) the value of the interest of the landlord in default determined on the assumption that the residential occupier continues to have the same right to occupy the premises as before that time; and*

(b) the value of that interest determined on the assumption that the residential occupier has ceased to have that right.

(2) In relation to any premises, any reference in this section to the interest of the landlord in default is a reference to his interest in the building in which the premises in question are comprised (whether or not that building contains any other premises) together with its curtilage.

(3) For the purposes of the valuations referred to in subsection (1) above, it shall be assumed—

(a) that the landlord in default is selling his interest on the open market to a willing buyer;

(b) that neither the residential occupier nor any member of his family wishes to buy; and

(c) that it is unlawful to carry out any substantial development of any of the land in which the landlord's interest subsists or to demolish the whole or part of any building on that land.

(4) In this section "the landlord in default" has the same meaning as in section 27 above and subsection (9) of that section applies in relation to this section as it applies in relation to that.

(5) Section 113 of the Housing Act 1985 (meaning of "members of a person's family") applies for the purposes of subsection (3)(b) above.

(6) The reference in subsection (3)(c) above to substantial development of any of the land in which the landlord's interest subsists is a reference to any development other than—

(a) development for which planning permission is granted by a general development order for the time being in force and which is carried out so as to comply with any condition or limitation subject to which planning permission is so granted; or

> *(b) a change of use resulting in the building referred to in subsection (2) above or any part of it being used as, or as part of, one or more dwelling-houses;*

> *and in this subsection "general development order" has the meaning given in section 56(6) of the Town and Country Planning Act 1990 and other expressions have the same meaning as in that Act."*

This section requires a court to calculate damages by reference to the difference between the value of the property if sold on the open market to a willing buyer assuming the tenant remained in situ on the same terms as immediately prior to him ceasing to occupy the property and the value of the property without the tenant in situ. The damages are therefore restitutionary. This calculation will inevitably require some valuation evidence which would ordinarily be provided by a valuation expert. The valuation is on a factual as opposed to a notional basis, otherwise the landlord would be ordered to pay the tenant a fine rather than the value of the profit occasioned by his wrongful acts: *Melville v Bruton* (1996) 29 HLR 319, CA.

In *Lambeth LBC v Loveridge* [2014] UKSC 65; [2015] HLR 12, the Supreme Court held that the fact that a person's status as a secure tenant would change on sale to a private buyer (in that case to an assured tenancy) was irrelevant to the assessment of a market value because the assumption in s.27(1)(a), i.e. that the residential occupier continues to have the same right to occupy the premises as before he ceased to occupy them, displaced it.

Importantly, a tenant who pursues a s.27 claim and a claim for reinstatement must elect between the two remedies at trial. An election to accept damages would mean that his tenancy would be deemed to have come to an end when he was unlawfully evicted: see *Osei-Bonsu v Wandsworth London Borough Council* [1999] 1 WLR 1011 at page 1025 D-E.

If damages are awarded under s.28, that precludes damages for loss of occupation which may arise under another cause of action: s.27(5), HA 1988. So, general or aggravated damages for the loss of occupation will be set off against statutory damages: *Nwokorie v Mason* (1994) 26 HLR 60. Conversely, general damages for harassment will not: *Kaur (Kashmir) v Gill* Times, June 15, 1995. Exemplary damages are not awarded in addition to statutory damages: *Francis v Brown* (1998) 30 HLR 143.

An advisor must therefore grapple with which measure of damages is likely to give rise to the maximum amount. In cases where there is extensive security of tenure, applying the measure under s.28 is likely to give rise to a significant damages award (a sitting tenant with even a hypothetical continuing interest devalues the reversionary interest considerably). Conversely, an assured shorthold tenant is, in many cases, easily evicted lawfully and, as such, the damage that type of tenancy does to the reversion is minimal if any.

Damages for trespass – the alternative to s.28

The Court of Appeal decision in *Smith v Khan* [2018] EWCA Civ 1137; [2018] H.L.R. 31, is considered in Chapter 4 in relation to liability being extinguished by reinstatement. One of the surprising aspects of the judgment is the approach taken to determining the measure of damages at common law for trespass (s.28 did not apply as the tenant abandoned her claim for reinstatement as the landlord had re-let the flat by the time the court ordered it) and particularly the period for which those damages were payable. S argued at first instance that she was entitled to damages assessed at £200 per night for the unlawful eviction for the period from 15.4.15 to the date of judgment on 14.12.15 ("the period"). In support of the period it was argued that the tenancy was continuing or would have continued until judgment but for the unlawful eviction.

At first instance, so far as material, the judge found that the tenancy had not ended by either surrender or enforcement of a court order so she awarded: damages comprising £40 for each night S was out of possession for the period; £1,500 aggravated damages; £1,200 exemplary damages; and £500 for harassment. The total sum awarded was almost £15,000. S appealed to a Circuit Judge who gave an *ex tempore* judgment in which he increased general damages to £130 per day, payable for the period.

The judge reflected on the period for which damages were payable and corrected it to reflect a period from 15.4.15 to 30.6.15 (the date by which he considered K could have lawfully evicted S at the earliest opportunity). The judge therefore awarded £9,880 in general damages. S understandably requested a hearing on this issue at which she highlighted that the judge below had made a finding that there had been no implied surrender of the tenancy. The judge determined that (i) general damages were limited to the period ending with the date by which the landlord could lawfully recover possession; (ii) contrary to the finding below, there had been an implied surrender when S's husband had left the property for Scotland (because S had not sought to enforce her matrimonial home rights to preserve the tenancy in advance of him leaving under s.33(3), Family Law Act 1996); and (iii) as the only protection available to S in the circumstances was s.3, PEA 1977, the correct period for calculating damages was 28 days from the 15.4.15 (it appears that the judge accepted this was the earliest time by which K could have obtained a possession order and did not factor in the time it would take to enforce it). The judge gave judgment for £3,640 for general damages (the effect of which was to almost halve the award made at first instance).

S appealed to the Court of Appeal which found the following: (i) the tenancy was an assured shorthold tenancy, the contractual term of which (if not surrendered nor lawfully terminated by execution of a court order) would have ended on 30.6.15 and which would have continued thereafter as a statutory periodic tenancy under s.5(2), HA 1988. The tenancy remained assured for so long as S occupied it as the tenant's wife (see s.30, FLA 1996) but her rights were limited to those held by her husband: s.30(8)(b), FLA 1996. K failed to comply with the statutory requirements to recover possession whether under Part I, HA 1988 or s.3, PEA 1977. The only issue therefore was the quantum of S's loss.

The Court of Appeal held that there was no surrender of the tenancy by S's husband prior to her eviction on 15.4.15. However, the fact that S did not pursue her claim for reinstatement, coupled with her husband's failure to assert or enforce his rights as tenant after her eviction led to the conclusion that neither occupied the premises as their only or principle home at the expiry of the contractual term and the tenancy did not therefore continue by s.5(2), HA 1988. The Court found no basis for awarding damages beyond this point given S's occupation rights had ended and she had been out of possession since 15.4.15.

The Court refused to determine the period during which damages were payable by reference to the hypothetical date when the tenancy could lawfully have been brought to an end because K had not sought to end it in that manner (at [39]). The Court upheld the daily rate of general damages of £130 which was in line with what it said "might be called the current tariff for this kind of award" and compensated for both the letting value of the premises of which she had been deprived and the anxiety and distress associated with that deprivation. In so doing, the Court acknowledged that "[a]lthough the awards made in other cases cannot be treated as strict precedents and judges must feel free to base their awards on their own assessment of the damage which has been caused, they do indicate the value which has been placed by the courts in those cases on the additional factors [...] mentioned."

The decision raises several questions about how to approach assessing damages for trespass in unlawful eviction claims. Those of most importance to practitioners are set out below.

- First, the circumstances of the case appear novel, but the principles derived from the facts are of much broader application. Most private sector assured shorthold tenancies are for an initial fixed term. If an unscrupulous landlord evicts and relets prior to expiry of that term such that the tenant is out of possession with little prospect of being readmitted quickly, then damages would arguably only run until the end of the fixed term.

- Secondly, and following from the above, it seems contrary to the purpose of the legislation that K was able to benefit from:
    - the unlawful eviction,
    - his refusal to reinstate S,
    - reletting the property to thwart S's enforcement of an injunction for reinstatement (and no doubt obtain a rental income), and
    - failure to disclose to the court when it made the order for reinstatement that the property had been relet.
- Thirdly, the reference to the PEA 1977 not giving rise to a cause of action casts doubt on the correctness of *Warder*.
- Fourthly, there is a real tension between the normal measure of damages for trespass and the approach in this case. Causation appeared to proceed on the basis of what happened rather than what would have happened *but for* the eviction. It is hard to see how the tenancy would have ended at the expiry of the fixed term save in the circumstances of the eviction. If so, damages would have continued to be payable until (at the earliest) the moment the tenancy could have been lawfully terminated, though arguably for much longer (subject to S taking reasonable steps to mitigate) as the claim was for trespass.
- On the same point, whilst it may seem logical in tort to compensate only the unlawfulness of the eviction (which means considering what would have happened if the eviction had proceeded lawfully), as discussed above, the approach to ascertaining the measure of damages for trespass is both complex and nuanced. It is arguable that but for the trespass, S would have suffered no loss and yet her loss is a continuing one as a result of it (subject to remoteness and mitigation). Those acting for occupants will be heartened that there is now support

for abandoning the "hypothetical lawful eviction" as a means of capping damages for trespass.

It is regrettable that the case will not be considered by the Supreme Court and that both occupants and landlords will be left to wrap their heads around what the implications of *Smith* are for their case.

Mitigation

If, in proceedings to enforce a liability arising by virtue of s.27(3), HA 1988, it appears to the court:

a) that, prior to the event which gave rise to the liability, the conduct of the former residential occupier or any person living with him in the premises concerned was such that it is reasonable to mitigate the damages for which the landlord in default would otherwise be liable, or

b) that, before the proceedings were begun, the landlord in default offered to reinstate the former residential occupier in the premises in question and either it was unreasonable of the former residential occupier to refuse that offer or, if he had obtained alternative accommodation before the offer was made, it would have been unreasonable of him to refuse that offer if he had not obtained that accommodation,

the court may reduce the amount of damages which would otherwise be payable to such amount as it thinks appropriate: s.27(7).

Section 27(7) only applies where the damages are awarded under s.28 and has no application damages awarded at common law (i.e. for breach of covenant or trespass/nuisance): *Regency (UK) Ltd v Albu-Swalin Heartland Property Ltd* [2019] EWHC 3713 (QB).

In *Regalgrand v Dickerson* (1997) 29 HLR 620 the court at first instance took into account rent arrears and reduced the amount of damages under s.28, HA 1988 accordingly. This decision was upheld by the

Court of Appeal. It is clear that "conduct" includes breaches of tenancy and is not confined to more serious misfeasance.

Quantum of damages

Assessing quantum of damages for distress and inconvenience is necessarily an imprecise art, turning as it does on the particular facts of each case. Nonetheless, it may be in the light of the reference to the loosely termed "tariff" in *Smith* that a more structured approach to assessing the quantum of damages relating to unlawful eviction is adopted in future with even greater emphasis on arriving at a figure by reference to a daily rate between £100 and £300. Though this provides a degree of clarity as to approach, it risks becoming an artificial cap on a claimant's loss.

It is clear from *Smith* that there is some benefit to be derived from looking at the types of awards made in comparable cases.

In *Tagro v Carfane* [1991] 23 HLR 250, CA, the court awarded £31,000 under s.28 for an unlawful eviction. The tenant was an assured (not an assured shorthold) tenant. Contrast *Melville v Bruton* (1997) 29 H.L.R. 319, CA which concerned an assured shorthold tenancy, where an award of £500 was substituted on appeal.

In *Mehta v Royal Bank of Scotland* (2000) 32 HLR 45, the claim was for damages under s.28, HA 1988 and general, aggravated and exemplary damages for an eviction by a mortgagee in possession and its receiver's agent of a tenant of a room in a hotel to facilitate a quick sale. The value of the premises without the plaintiff in occupation was £800,000 which was the offer which the receiver accepted; a valuation based on nuisance value provided some assistance and on the basis of the evidence, a purchaser, if prepared to purchase at all, would have required a substantial discount of not less than £45,000. General damages for trespass to land and goods were ordered in the sum of £10,000; there had been exceptional conduct and motive on the part of the receiver and the managing agent acting on the landlord's behalf which was designed solely for profit and in the circumstances an award of £10,000 was appropriate; in addition, an award of £7,500 exemplary damages was appropriate owing to the urgency with which possession of the premises were required. These damages were set off against the s.28 award.

In *Choudhury v Garcia* [2013] EWHC 3283 (QB), in a case for unlawful eviction from a ground-floor room in a house which C required for his ill wife and in breach of stay of execution pending an appeal against the making of a possession order, a judge ordered C to pay to G special damages in the sum of £2,203; general damages in the sum of £7,000; exemplary damages in the sum of £5,000, and damages for harassment in the sum of £1,800.

In *Albu-Swalin* (above), A had been an assured shorthold tenant of a flat which he occupied with his son. His landlord served a defective s.21 notice on him and he did not leave the flat. The landlord evicted him by changing the locks and his possessions were disposed of. He was awarded damages of £150 per day for 60 days (representing the notice period he ought to have been given). He was also awarded £1,000 aggravated damages, £5,000 special damages for his lost possessions and £4,000 exemplary damages.

Recent decisions in the county court

Although not binding (and to an extent) only marginally persuasive, decisions of the county court do provide a guide to the level of damages being awarded for unlawful eviction and harassment claims. Two recent county court decisions which illustrate the variance in awards for unlawful eviction and harassment are summarised below. A compendium of such county court decisions can be found in Quiet Enjoyment, Protection from Rogue Landlords, 8th ed.

In *Sanchez v Simple Properties Management Ltd*, Legal Action April 2020, County Court at Central London, a case including claims of unlawful eviction and harassment, the court made an award *inter alia* of (1) £18,000 general damages assessed at £200 per day for the period of 90 days (the period ending with the earliest date the tenancy could be ended lawfully), during which time she had slept on a friend's floor; (2) £2,000 exemplary damages; (3) £2,000 aggravated damages; and (5)

£8,800 for harassment (falling toward the upper end of the lower band in *Vento v Chief Constable of West Yorkshire Police* [2002] EWCA Civ 1871. The court applied a 10% uplift to the general damages (it is unclear whether this uplift was applied to the adjusted *Vento*-based damages which are already uplifted under the Presidential Guidance referred to above).

In *ZN v BA*, Legal Action June 2019, County Court at Central London, ZN was an assured shorthold tenancy of a flat. BA was his landlord. In October and again in November 2015, BA disabled the boiler such that ZN had no heating or hot water. It was restored only after the local authority intervened. BA again disabled the boiler in December 2015 for six months at which time the boiler was replaced. ZN was awarded £10,650 (general damages).

POINTS TO NOTE

- **Damages for breach of contract are very likely to be less in cases of unlawful eviction and harassment than in tort. Practitioners should always look to rely on a cause of action in tort such as trespass or nuisance in addition to a contractual cause of action.**

- **Damages for harassment are conventionally assessed according to the "*Vento*" bands. In a typical unlawful eviction case with associated harassment, this is likely to result in a general damages award for injury to feelings in the "less serious" category.**

- **Collating evidence about loss and damage early on is essential for three reasons: first because receipts for goods go missing and bank statements are never suitably clear as to what has been purchased; secondly, memory regarding distress and inconvenience fades over time (and is often tempered); and thirdly, the better idea a claimant has as to the likely damages** to be awarded, the more likely meaningful negotiation is to achieve settlement and Part 36 offers can be made.

- Damages under s.28, HA 1988 are not available where a tenant is reinstated to the premises (but that should not prevent it being pleaded in the alternative where reinstatement is not guaranteed – it can always be abandoned later).

- Damages under s.28, HA 1988 depend on valuation evidence.

- Aggravated and exemplary damages must be pleaded so do not forget to include them in the Claim Form and Particulars of Claim.

- Exemplary damages are not available where an award is made under s.28, HA 1988 and aggravated damages are set off against such an award.

- The measure of damages for unlawful eviction has been considered by the Court of Appeal in *Smith v Khan* (above); it importantly makes clear that damages for trespass continue for the period the tenancy actually subsists and not by reference to a hypothetical lawful termination of the tenancy where possession proceedings would have been taken.

CHAPTER SEVEN
INJUNCTIONS AND UNDERTAKINGS

As has already been seen in Chapter 5, there are specific statutory causes of action which enable a person to claim for an injunction restraining harassing conduct by another person: s.3 and 3A, PHA 1997. Injunctions are also available for breach of contract and where a tort has been committed (Chapters 2 to 4). This chapter examines, from a practical perspective, the use of injunctions as a remedy in claims for unlawful eviction, i.e. to prevent eviction or harassment, for reinstatement to the property or for delivery up of belongings. Again, it is presumed that such claims would be brought in the County Court.

An injunction is a discretionary remedy granted by the court which can prohibit or compel conduct by the person against whom it is granted. The former is called a "prohibitory injunction" and the latter a "mandatory injunction". Section 37 of the Senior Courts Act 1981 provides the High Court with what is now a statutory power to grant injunctions where it is "just and convenient to do so". The power to grant an injunction is unlimited but whether and how it is granted is governed by previous binding case law and the rules of court: *Fourie v Le Roux* [2007] UKHL 1; [2007] 1 W.L.R. 320.

Section 38 of the County Courts Act 1984 confers a general power, subject to regulations, for the County Court to make any order which could be made by the High Court if the proceedings were heard there including an injunction.

Injunctions can be granted as a final remedy at the conclusion of a claim or an interim remedy designed to "hold the line" thus preventing further wrongdoing pending the outcome of the trial. Both types of remedy are considered below and there are different tests which apply to the grant of either. In a claim for unlawful eviction and/or harassment, it is very likely that some form of interim relief will need to be considered if not actually sought and a final injunction is likely to be necessary if an occupant is reinstated and does not want to be unlawfully evicted or harassed again in future.

Who can grant injunctions?

The application notice requires the applicant to specify the judge who should hear the application. A District Judge may hear an application for an injunction under s.3, PHA 1997 including an application for an interim remedy: CPR PD 2B, para.8.1(c)(ii). Otherwise, unless prevented by statute, a rule or practice direction, a District Judge can hear any matter which could be heard by a District Judge in the High Court: CPR PD 2B, para.8.1. This includes a claim for unlawful eviction and any related application for an interim injunction: CPR PD 25 para.1.3. An application for an order varying or discharging an injunction or an undertaking given to the court may be allocated to a District Judge: CPR PD 2B, para.8.2.

When can injunctions be granted?

It was recently confirmed that generally, in order to obtain an injunction (whether final or interim), the person seeking it must be able to show a cause of action (i.e. a recognised claim for a remedy in e.g. contract or tort). Injunctions are not freestanding remedies and there must be a claim recognised in law to which it attaches: see *Octagon Overseas Ltd and another v Coates* [2017] EWHC 877 (Ch) [2017] EWHC 877 (Ch); [2017] H.L.R. 26.

INTERIM INJUNCTIONS

A court can grant an interim injunction and an interim remedy under s.4, T(I)GA 1977: CPR r.25.1. As an alternative, a court can accept an undertaking from a defendant as to his future conduct.

In order to obtain an interim injunction to prevent eviction, harassment or conversion or disposal of goods, a claimant must show that the "balance of convenience" weighs in favour of the grant of relief. To do that he must show:

- there is a serious issue to be tried between the parties (i.e. a serious dispute);
- that damages would prove an inadequate remedy; and
- that the narrower balance of convenience (or justice) lies with making the injunction sought: *American Cyanamid Co v Ethicon Ltd* [1975] AC 396.

Serious dispute

A serious issue to be tried is one where there is material disclosing a dispute exists and the outcome is uncertain: *Cayne v Global Natural Resources plc* [1984] 1 All ER 225, CA.

If the defendant accepts that he has unlawfully evicted the claimant (or would do) then there is no serious dispute between the parties and a final (as opposed to interim) injunction should be granted.

Adequacy of damages

If the defendant denies the allegations, then the court moves on to consider whether damages would adequately compensate the claimant (this is highly unlikely to be the case where unlawful eviction or harassment takes place owing to the distress and inconvenience caused).

Cross-undertakings

The court will also assess whether a cross-undertaking to pay the defendant damages in the event the interim injunction is found to have been wrongly granted should be given. This type of undertaking is often worded along the lines of "*If the court later finds that this order has caused loss to the Respondent and decides that the Respondent should be compensated for that loss, the Applicant will comply with any order the court may make.*"

It is critical for advisors to inform claimants that they are likely to be required to give a cross-undertaking in damages to the defendant. The loss most likely to be suffered by a landlord if it is found that an interim injunction is wrongly granted in an unlawful eviction case is the loss of profit from reletting the premises at a higher rent.

If a claimant is without funds, that is not in itself a bar to an order being granted: see *Allen v Jambo Holdings Ltd* [1980] 1 WLR 1252 (where a legally aided applicant provided an undertaking of questionable value).

Balance of justice

Thus, in most disputed cases of unlawful eviction or harassment, the real issue will be where the balance of justice lies. This involves consideration of what the effect of making the injunction will be on each party and looking at all the circumstances in the round. Whilst the courts have often referred to the need for a claimant to show *a prima facie case* or *reasonable prospects of success*, this inflexible approach has been criticised and held not to be consistent with *American Cyanamid*: *Epoch Co Ltd v Character Options Ltd* [2015] EWHC 3436 (IPEC).

> "*The extent to which the disadvantages to each party would be incapable of being compensated in damages in the event of his succeeding at the trial is always a significant factor in assessing where the balance of convenience lies; and if the extent of the uncompensatable disadvantage to each party would not differ widely, it may not be improper to take into account in tipping the balance the relative strength of each party's case as revealed by the affidavit evidence adduced on the hearing of the application. This, however, should be done only where it is apparent upon the facts disclosed by evidence as to which there is no credible dispute that the strength of one party's case is disproportionate to that of the other party. The court is not justified in embarking upon anything resembling a trial of the action upon conflicting affidavits in order to evaluate the strength of either*

party's case.": *American Cyanamid per* Lord Diplock (at p.409A-C).

Thus, whilst some weight could be given to the merits either way, the court should not look to conduct a mini trial of the issues.

Mandatory injunctions

It was thought that the *American Cyanamid* principles required special application in the context of mandatory injunctions: see e.g. *Nottingham Building Society v Eurodynamics Systems Plc* [1993] FSR 486; applied in *Zockoll Group Ltd v Mercury Communications Ltd* [1998] F.S.R. 354; and recently in *Harmony Innovation Shipping PTE Ltd v Caravel Shipping Inc.* [2019] EWHC 1037 (Comm), where it was held that an interim injunction will be granted for delivery up where:

- there is a high degree of assurance that the applicant will be successful at trial; and
- the risk of injustice if the injunction is not granted outweighs such a risk if it is granted.

However, in the Privy Council decision of *National Commercial Bank Jamaica v Olint Corp Ltd* [2009] UKPC 16; [2009] Bus. L.R. 1110, Lord Hoffman held the following:

- At the interim stage, a court must assess whether granting or withholding an injunction is more likely to produce a just result (at [16]).
- In practice, it is often hard to tell whether either damages or the cross-undertaking will be an adequate remedy. The basic principle is that the court should take whichever course seems likely to cause the least irremediable prejudice to one party or the other (at [17]).
- Amongst other things, the court may take into account the prejudice which the parties will suffer whether or not an injunction

is made; the likelihood of such prejudice actually occurring; the extent to which it may be compensated by an award of damages or enforcement of the cross-undertaking; the likelihood of either party being able to satisfy such an award; and the likelihood that the injunction will turn out to have been wrongly granted or withheld, that is to say, the court's opinion of the relative strength of the parties' cases (at [18]).

- In both mandatory and prohibitory cases, the underlying principle is the same, namely, that the court should take whichever course seems likely to cause the least irremediable prejudice to one party or the other: R v Secretary of State for Transport, Ex p Factortame Ltd (No 2) [1991] 1 AC 603, pp.682–683.

- The box-ticking approach of categorising an injunction as mandatory or prohibitory and then applying a rule that if it was mandatory, a "high degree of assurance" was required, while if it was prohibitory, all that was needed was a "serious issue to be tried" does not do justice to the complexity of a decision as to whether or not to grant an interim injunction.

- In each case a court must examine what on the particular facts of the case the consequences of granting or withholding of the injunction is likely to be. If it appears that the injunction is likely to cause irremediable prejudice to the defendant (which is more likely to be the case in an application for a mandatory injunction) a court may be reluctant to grant it unless satisfied that the chances that it will turn out to have been wrongly granted are low; that is to say, that the court will feel "a high degree of assurance that at the trial it will appear that the injunction was rightly granted".

The *Olint* decision has been followed in several recent authorities including *Evalve Inc. v Edwards Lifesciences Ltd.* [2019] EWHC 1158 (Pat); [202] FSR 4; *Unite the Union v Birmingham CC* [2019] EWHC 992 (QB) and *WH Holding Ltd. v E20 Stadium LLP* [2018] EWHC 2367 (Ch).

Harassment and threatened eviction

In a case involving harassment or threats to evict, the balance of justice will almost certainly fall in favour of preserving the status quo and permitting the occupant to remain in the premises without harassment pending the outcome of the trial.

Where rent arrears are in issue (as is common), a court would ordinarily require rent (or an occupation charge, if the status of the occupant as a tenant is in issue) to be paid whilst the proceedings are ongoing – albeit the grant or continuation of an injunction is unlikely to be contingent on that occurring and the landlord should be expected to take whatever lawful action is available to him in respect of those arrears in the meantime, including commencing possession proceedings without prejudice to any defence he may have as to the need to take them.

Reinstatement

In cases where a mandatory order is sought for reinstatement as the claimant has been evicted, the approach is the same as in *American Cyanamid* but if it appears that the injunction is likely to cause irremediable prejudice to the defendant (which is more likely in an application for a mandatory injunction) the court may want to satisfy itself to a high degree of assurance that at the trial it will appear that the injunction was rightly granted: *Nottingham Building Society v Eurodynamics Systems Plc* and *Olint* (above).

Where the defendant denies that the claimant is entitled to reinstatement and has installed a new tenant it is likely that interim relief will be refused. Where a defendant accepts the claimant is entitled to be reinstated but the premises have been re-let, the court should make a declaration that the claimant is entitled to possession as against the new tenants and (if the claimant is so minded) give directions for those tenants to be joined for the purposes of claiming possession against them: *Love v Herrity* (1991) 23 HLR 217. In cases where reinstatement is actively and appropriately pursued, this is without question the approach that should now be taken in the light of the decision in *Smith v Khan* [2018] EWCA Civ 1137; [2018] H.L.R. 31, where the Court of

Appeal found that a failure to pursue reinstatement (where the landlord had relet the premises) ultimately (and in conjunction with other matters) served to reduce the amount of damages available to the claimant. It is imperative that a claimant seeking to preserve the ongoing occupation arrangement take steps to enforce his right to possession or risk a court finding that it has been impliedly surrendered by conduct.

Undertakings

An undertaking is a promise to the court to do or refrain from doing specified acts. In the context of unlawful eviction and harassment, it takes the place of an injunction order but is capable of enforcement in the same way. It does not depend on the making of any concessions by the person giving it nor does it require the court to make findings of fact. It is often a means of reaching a holding position pending determination of the substantive claim at trial.

An undertaking is ordinarily provided using Form N117. The court may refuse to accept the undertaking unless the person giving it has signed a statement to the effect that he or she understands the terms of the undertaking and the consequences of failure to comply: CPR PD 81, para.2.2.

It is a fundamental principle that undertakings must be complied with. A person who has given an undertaking to the court is under a plain and unqualified obligation to comply to the letter with his undertaking. Where, as in the present case, the undertaking is to do something by a specified time, then time is of the essence. A person who finds himself unable to comply timeously with his undertaking should apply for an extension of time before the time for compliance has expired. It is simply not acceptable to put forward — least of all for a solicitor to put forward — as an explanation for non-compliance with an undertaking the burden of other work. This obligation applies irrespective of any views which those who have given the undertaking may have as to its appropriateness or validity: *R (Bempoa) v Southwark LBC* [2002] EWHC 153 (Admin); [2002] NPC 23.

PROCEDURE

The procedure for making an underlying claim for unlawful eviction, harassment and any other relief is considered in Chapter 10. What follows below is that procedure governing the making of an application for an interim injunction whether before or after a claim has commenced.

Generally, an order for an interim injunction may be made at any time, including before proceedings are started (i.e. where a claim form has been issued) and after judgment has been given: CPR r.25.1. However, the court may grant an interim remedy before a claim has been made only if the matter is urgent or it is otherwise desirable to do so in the interests of justice: CPR r.25.2. Where it grants an interim remedy before a claim has been commenced, the court should give directions requiring a claim to be commenced: CPR r.25.3.

An application for an interim remedy must be supported by evidence, unless the court orders otherwise: CPR r.25.3(2).

On notice applications

To commence an application for an injunction on three working days' notice to the defendant, in addition to filing the Claim Form and Particulars of Claim (where possible), save for cases of extreme urgency (see below), the applicant must file at court a completed N16A application form, a draft form of order (including all the matters referred to in CPR PD 25A at paras.2.1-2.4) and a witness statement in support (including exhibits).

The application notice must state the order sought, and the date, time and place of the hearing. A completed Form N16A and evidence in support must be served as soon as practicable after issue and in any event not less than three working days before the court is due to hear the application: CPR PD 25A, paras.2.1 and 2.2. Sufficient copies of the documents should be sent to the court where it is envisaged the court will serve the other parties: CPR PD 25A, para.2.3. In cases involving two parties only, this will normally mean three copies (the other being for the court file).

A draft of the order sought should be filed with the application notice and a disk containing the draft should also be available to the court in a format compatible with the word processing software used by the court. This will enable the court officer to arrange for any amendments to be incorporated and for the speedy preparation and sealing of the order: CPR PD 25A, para.2.4. Often the courts are willing to accept an email from solicitors addressed to that court's "hearings@" email address which contains a draft of the order. If in doubt, contact the court beforehand to find out what processes are in place for this to happen.

Evidence generally

Applications for other interim injunctions must be supported by evidence set out in either a witness statement, or the application/a statement of case provided that it is verified by a statement of truth, unless the court, an Act, a rule or a practice direction requires evidence by affidavit: CPR PD 25A, para 3.2. See CPR Part 32 for more information on the format and content of witness statements and Part 22 for details of statements of truth.

The evidence must set out the facts on which the applicant relies for the claim being made against the respondent, including all material facts of which the court should be made aware: CPR PD 25A, para 3.3.

Service

The claimant should be prepared (especially in the defendant's absence) to prove that the application notice and supporting documents have been served on the defendant (usually by provision of a completed Certificate of Service – form N215).

Without notice applications

By CPR r.25.3, the court may grant an interim remedy on an application made without notice if it appears to the court that there are good reasons for not giving notice. The application must be supported by evidence and that evidence must address the reasons why notice has not been provided: CPR r.25.3(4); CPR PD 25A, para.3.4.

In *Olint* (above), Lord Hoffman stated that a judge should not entertain an application for an injunction, without notice to the defendant, unless either no time was available to give notice (which is in fact often not the case) or notice would give the defendant the opportunity to take steps to defeat the purpose of the injunction (as in the case of a search order or freezing injunction). See also *RST v UVW* [2009] EWHC 2448 (QB); [2010] EMLR 13 (at [7]).

It is open to argument whether fear of reprisals or escalation of conduct in the context of an unlawful eviction and harassment claim would fall within this category. The purpose of the injunction would not be *defeated* by giving notice, it would give rise to a peremptory breach which arguably is not the same thing.

That the issue of whether to proceed without notice on grounds of secrecy should be considered in any case for without notice relief is illustrated in *Birmingham CC v Afsar* [2019] EWHC 1560 (QB); [2019] E.L.R. 373 the combination of the need to justify secrecy and the duty of full and frank disclosure (discussed below) means any application for a without notice injunction must "provide the Court with a distinct, clear, and sufficient explanation, founded upon evidence, for making its application without notice to any of the defendants, identifying the counter-arguments which could be put forward, and explaining why those arguments should not be accepted": *Asfar* (at [55]).

Urgent applications and applications without notice

Where an application for urgent relief if made (whether before issue of the claim form or afterwards) and no notice of the application is given to the other parties, the following approach applies. Such applications are normally dealt with at a court hearing, but cases of extreme urgency may be dealt with by telephone: CPR PD 25A, para.4.2.

Applications dealt with at a court hearing

Where the application is dealt with at a court hearing after issue of a claim form:

- The application notice, evidence in support and a draft order should be filed with the court two hours before the hearing wherever possible: CPR PD 25A, para.4.3(1).
- If an application is made before the application notice has been issued, a draft order should be provided at the hearing, and the application notice and evidence in support must be filed with the court on the same or next working day or as ordered by the court: CPR PD 25A, para.4.3(2).
- Except in cases where secrecy is essential, the applicant should take steps to notify the respondent informally of the application: CPR PD 25A, para.4.3(3). This could be by email, telephone or even text message/via social media direct messaging. Practitioners often confuse the need for secrecy with the need to protect the claimant from repercussions if the defendant knows of the application. The decision in *Olint*, above, should be borne in mind in this regard.

Applications made before the issue of a claim form

In addition to the provisions set out at 4.3 above, where an application is made before issue of the claim:

- Unless the court orders otherwise, either the applicant must undertake to the court to issue a claim form immediately or the court will give directions for the commencement of the claim: CPR PD 25A, para.4.4(1).
- Where possible the claim form should be served with the order for the injunction: CPR PD 25A, para.4.4(2).

- An order made before the issue of a claim form should state in the title after the names of the applicant and respondent 'the Claimant and Defendant in an Intended Action': CPR PD 25A, para.4.4(3).

Applications by telephone

These applications are governed by CPR PD 25, para.4.5 which provides the following:

- Injunctions will be heard by telephone only where the applicant is acting by counsel or solicitors. This should be appreciated, and appropriate steps taken to secure such attendance: CPR PD 25A, para.4.5(5).

- Where the facility is available it is likely that the judge will require a draft order to be faxed to him. In practice, many judges now accept receipt of drafts by email: CPR PD 25A, para.4.5(3).

- Where it is not possible to arrange a hearing, application can be made between 10.00 a.m. and 5.00 p.m. weekdays by telephoning the Royal Courts of Justice on 020 7947 6000 and asking to be put in contact with a High Court Judge of the appropriate Division available to deal with an emergency application in a High Court matter. The appropriate district registry may also be contacted by telephone. In county court proceedings, the appropriate County Court hearing centre should be contacted: CPR PD 25A, para.4.5(1).

- Where an application is made outside those hours the applicant should either

(a) telephone the Royal Courts of Justice on 020 7947 6000 where he will be put in contact with the clerk to the appropriate duty judge in the High Court (or the appropriate area Circuit Judge where known), or

(b) the Urgent Court Business Officer of the appropriate Circuit who will contact the local duty judge: CPR PD 25, para.4.5(2).

- The application notice and evidence in support must be filed with the court on the same or next working day or as ordered, together with two copies of the order for sealing: CPR PD 25A, para.4.5(4).

Full and frank disclosure

The duty of full and frank disclosure of all material facts within the claimant's (and his lawyers') knowledge applies to all applications made without notice: *Castelli v Cook* (1849) 7 Hare 89, 94; *Rex v Kensington Income Tax Commissioners, Ex parte de Polignac (Princess)* [1917] 1 KB 486, 509.

The duty extends to disclosing all facts which could reasonably be considered material by the judge (not the applicant), presenting the case fully and fairly, providing witness evidence which summarises the case and evidence for both sides (not burying adverse material in exhibits which are not then drawn out in the body of the statement), investigating the nature of the claim and facts relied on before applying and identifying any likely defences as well as then advancing to the court the key points for and against the application: *Marc Rich & Co Holding GmbH v Krasner* [1999] CLY 487). The duty continues until the injunction order becomes operative (i.e. when it is personally served). The duty includes providing a full note of hearing to the defendant and any other affected party whether or not it is requested: *Interoute Telecommunications (UK) Ltd v Fashion Gossip Ltd*, The Times, November 10, 1999 (Lightman J).

Material non-disclosure may result in the injunction being discharged (*see Asfar* (above)) and risks professional misconduct in the case of legal representatives).

The hearing

The representatives for the parties should endeavour to provide a skeleton argument in support or opposition (where relevant) to the application. This ensures two things: first that all material points are in writing (particularly important in the context of a without notice application); and secondly, assuming the judge has time to read them prior to calling the parties in, that the hearing can proceed swiftly.

At the hearing of a without notice injunction, the duty of full and frank disclosure continues. Anything which may have been discovered since the issue of the claim or application should be put before the judge. In these circumstances, it is incumbent on a representative for the claimant to ensure the judge deals with the matter thoroughly. There can be a temptation to whittle through the papers swiftly, particularly if the matter is inserted into a busy list, but this approach should be avoided and every effort made to ensure the absent party's case is before the court and fairly presented. The court should set a return date for the application to be heard on notice and do so within a short space of time (usually a matter of days).

In an on-notice hearing, the court will hear argument from both sides on the respective merits of the application (applying the approach above in *American Cyanamid*). The court should not need to hear evidence as the argument turns on whether there is a serious issue to be tried but it has been known for a claimant to be questioned about his ability to satisfy a cross-undertaking at an on-notice hearing. It should be apparent to advisors whether such matters will be in issue at an on-notice hearing and steps taken to ensure that the point can be addressed in a way the court considers is in the interests of justice and proportionate. For those responding to an application, it will be advantageous to have prepared a witness statement in response to the application, dealing particularly with those matters which are in dispute (if any), the ability of the respondent to give an undertaking in damages, any steps the respondent is willing to take to mitigate against the need for an injunction (including a willingness to give undertakings as to his conduct) and any evidence which goes to the justice of the case.

Injunction orders

CPR PD 25A, paras.5.1-5.5 identify those matters which must, unless the court orders otherwise, be contained in any order for an injunction. They are:

- A clear statement of what the injunction prohibits or requires the respondent to do;
- The applicant's cross undertaking in damages;
- The applicant's undertaking, where the application is made without notice, to serve on the respondent as soon as practicable the application notice, evidence in support and any order
- a return date (where the application is made without notice);
- The applicant's undertaking (where the application is made before the filing of an application notice) to file the application and pay the appropriate fee on same or next working day;
- The applicant's undertaking (where the application is made before the claim form is issued) to issue the claim and pay the appropriate fee on same or next working day; or directions for commencement of claim.

The order must be worded so that the person subject to it knows precisely what he is to be prevented from doing or required to do: Lawrence David v Ashton [1989] I.C.R. 123.

Service of an order once obtained

Once an order has been obtained, to ensure it can be enforced by committal proceedings it must be served personally on the defendant unless substituted service has been permitted: CPR r.81.6 and r.81.8(2)(b).

In the event of non-compliance with the terms of the order, the claimant can apply to court for the defendant's committal: see Chapter 8.

Applications to vary or discharge

A respondent served with an injunction made in his absence can apply to vary or discharge it: CPR r.3.1(7). Where the injunction is made without notice, a swift return date should have been included on the order which will provide an opportunity for the respondent to be heard without the need for a formal application to vary or discharge the injunction. This should also be the case where the application is made on short notice. In any other case (i.e. where the respondent was on notice), any application should be made promptly and address any material change of circumstances or facts relied on which were overlooked in genuine error: *Tibbles v SIG Plc (t/a Asphaltic Roofing Supplies)* [2012] EWCA Civ 518. Where possible, the application should be supported by a witness statement from the applicant.

POINTS OF NOTE

- **Advisors should assess whether an undertaking might be an acceptable holding position on an interim basis, rather than an injunction. This may not be acceptable in a harassment-type case where the application for a warrant is contingent on the court having granted the injunction, however it would not prevent a paper committal application being brought against the alleged contemnor.**

- **A without notice application for an injunction is inappropriate unless either no time is available to give notice (which is in fact often not the case) or notice would give the defendant the opportunity to take steps to defeat the purpose of the injunction. The need for secrecy is one reason for an application being made without notice but where relied on, the application must provide distinct, clear, and sufficient explan-**

ation, founded upon evidence, identifying the counter-arguments which could be put forward, and explaining why those arguments should not be accepted. It is no longer sufficient to make a bare assertion that an occupant fears reprisal.

- Short notice should be given wherever possible, whether by telephone call, text message or email.
- The duty to provide full and frank disclosure on without notice injunctions is incredibly important and must be fulfilled.
- The requirements for inclusion in injunction order should be observed strictly. The absence of any one where necessary may result in arguments regarding the applicant's ability to enforce the order.
- A respondent's application to vary or discharge should be made promptly.

CHAPTER EIGHT
COMMITTAL PROCEEDINGS

This chapter provides a practical overview of how to tackle a defendant's failure to comply with the terms of an injunction or undertaking preventing eviction, for reinstatement, or for delivery up of the claimant's belongings. Where a court order which contains a penal notice is breached, the court has power to punish the person in breach ("the contemnor") through a process known as "committal". This is not to be confused with committal in the criminal procedure context. It is the means by which a judge can fine, imprison or seize a contemnor's goods for a contempt of court.

The County Court's power to commit for contempt of court is derived from s.38, County Court 1984 (which confers the powers of the High Court) and the Senior Courts Act 1981

In order to clarify and consolidate the provisions of the Rules of Supreme Court ("RSC"), Ord.52 with parts of RSC Ord.45 and the County Court Rules Ord.29, Part 81 of the CPR was introduced (along with a corresponding practice direction). It applies in the County Court as well as the High Court and the Court of Appeal. It concerns only procedure and not the law regarding committal. Advisors should therefore familiarise themselves with CPR Part 81 and PD 81 wherever committal proceedings are contemplated.

The purpose of the court's jurisdiction for contempt of court is to uphold the rule of law by protecting or enforcing the authority of the court. Resort should be had to its salutary but draconian powers only where there is no other effective means of achieving the desired objective. It not be used as a tool of oppression or even as a tactical weapon: *The Lakah Group v Al Jazeera Satellite Channel* [2002] EWHC 2500 (QB).

Breach of the injunction

It is for the person applying to commit the contemnor for breach of the injunction to prove the breach: *Mubarak v Mubarak* [2001] 1 FLR 698. The burden of proof is the criminal standard (beyond reasonable doubt): *Phillips v Symes* [2003] EWCA Civ 1769; *Sarayiah v Williams* [2018] EWHC 324 (QB) and PD 81.9.

Intention

Liability for civil contempt for breach of an injunction does not depend upon establishing any specific intention either to breach the terms of the order or to subvert the administration of justice in general: *Stancomb v Trowbridge UDC* [1910] 2 Ch 190, at 194; *A-G v Times Newspapers Ltd* [1992] 1 AC 191 at 217 per Lord Oliver. All that is necessary is that the contemnor understood that an order was made forbidding them to do certain things and that, if they did them, they may well be punished: *P v P (Contempt of Court: Mental Capacity)* [1999] 2 F.L.R. 897.

However, the applicant should assess whether the acts which it is said breach the terms of the injunction or undertaking actually do fall within its terms. Whether or not a particular act amounts to "harassment" for example is up for debate if an alleged contemnor asserts that a course of conduct is required for such a breach to occur and they perpetrated only one act. Whether a person has reinstated or evicted a tenant e.g. will be much easier to ascertain.

Penal notices in injunction orders and undertakings

In order to commit a person for breach of a court order (or undertaking) the order itself should contain what is known as a "penal notice": CPR r.81.9; 81PD 1. This is "a warning to the person required to do or not do the act in question that disobedience to the order would be a contempt of court punishable by imprisonment, a fine or sequestration of assets". The form of words is currently as follows (or in words to substantially the same effect):

"If you the within-named [ ] do not comply with this order you may be held to be in contempt of court and imprisoned or fined, or your assets may be seized."

Advisors should note that the reference to assets being seized is a relatively recent addition and any template forms should be checked for compliance with the above wording.

If an order or undertaking does not contain a penal notice, for whatever reason, the court can waive the requirement for one if the court is satisfied that no injustice would be caused to the respondent (e.g. where he already knows of the possible consequences of breach). The alternative is an application to add a penal notice to the order whereby any subsequent breach would be capable of being enforced by committal proceedings.

Service of the order

By CPR r.81.5(1), unless the court dispenses with service under r.81.8, a judgment or order may not be enforced by committal proceedings unless a copy of it has been served on the person required to do or not do the act in question, and in the case of a judgment or order requiring a person to do an act (such as reinstating an occupant):

- the copy has been served before the end of the time fixed for doing the act, together with a copy of any order fixing that time;
- where the time for doing the act has been varied by a subsequent order or agreement under CPR r.2.11, a copy of that subsequent order or agreement has also been served personally (CPR r.81.6); and
- where the judgment or order was made under CPR r.81.4(5), or was made pursuant to an earlier judgment or order requiring the act to be done, a copy of the earlier judgment or order has also been served.

Copies of undertakings

Copies of undertakings given by a defendant are served by the court delivering a copy to the person who gave it:

- by handing to that person a copy of the document before that person leaves the court building;
- by posting a copy to that person at the residence or place of business of that person where this is known; or
- by posting a copy to that person's solicitor: CPR r.81.7.

If delivery cannot happen in accordance with the above, a copy of the undertaking will be provided to the party for whose benefit it was given for them to effect personal service as soon as practicable. In reality, where an undertaking is given, the court directs a respondent to wait within the court building until a copy of the undertaking can be handed to him by the court clerk.

Dispensation with personal service

A court can dispense with the requirement for personal service of the order where it is satisfied the defendant has had notice of it by being present when it was made or by being notified of its terms by telephone, email or otherwise: CPR r.81.8(1). This will be particularly relevant where e.g. an urgent injunction preventing an imminent eviction or for reinstatement has been obtained where the defendant did not attend. Practitioners should endeavour to include within the draft order dispensation of the need for personal service on condition that the defendant is notified of the content of the order by telephone, email or other suitable means of communication and a copy is thereafter served on him.

In most cases however, it is best to try and effect personal service if the defendant is not present in court when the order is made. This will go some way towards avoiding satellite arguments on committal regarding whether the defendant knew of the terms of the order.

Application

Assuming the order to be enforced complies with the above requirements, and has been properly served, the claimant is at liberty to enforce it by an application to commit an alleged contemnor for breach of its terms.

Specific rules relating to order for delivery up of goods

There are specific rules relating to orders requiring delivery up of goods of which advisers should be aware before making an application to commit the defendant for breach of that order.

By CPR 81.4(5) if a judgment or order requires a person to deliver goods or pay their value the judgment or order cannot be enforced by a committal order under CPR r.81.4(1); the person entitled to enforce the judgment or order may apply to the court for an order requiring that the goods be delivered *within a specified time*; and, where the court grants such an order, that order may be enforced in the usual way.

Other cases

In the case of orders made pursuant to the pre-conditions in CPR r.81.4(5) and otherwise, the procedure for applying to commit for contempt of court is as follows.

A committal application is made by an application notice under CPR, Part 23 (whether in the context of ongoing proceedings or against a third party to those proceedings): r.81.10(1), (2).

The application notice must address the following:

- It must state that the application is made in the proceedings in question, and its title and reference number must correspond with the title and reference number of those proceedings: CPR PD 81, para.13.1;

- It must set out in full the grounds on which the committal application is made and must identify, separately and numerically, each alleged act of contempt including, if known, the date of each of the alleged acts; CPR r.81.10(3)(a). Practitioners should use a schedule to record the allegations, depicting in columns: the date, time, allegation, reference to evidence proving the allegation, and the term of the injunction that the allegation is said to have breached.

- It must be supported by one or more affidavits containing *all* the evidence relied upon: r.81.10(3)(b). The reference to *all* evidence should be noted. It cannot be the case that relevant and probative evidence which comes to light only after the committal application has been made would be excluded under this rule. It is the author's view that the evidence *relied upon* must be assessed at the time of the application. This means that any evidence which was available at the time of the application but omitted might be excluded unless the court waives the non-compliance.

Practitioners are reminded that the standard of proof for applicants in committal proceedings is beyond reasonable doubt. To avoid any applications to strike out because the evidence is incapable of satisfying that burden (e.g. it is all anonymous hearsay) the strength of evidence in support of committal should be assessed at the outset and appropriate advice given on merits.

The application notice and the evidence in support must be served personally on the respondent but the court may dispense with such service if it considers it just to do so; or make an order in respect of service by an alternative method or at an alternative place: CPR r.81.10(4), (5).

Where a committal application is commenced by an application notice:

- An amendment to the application notice may be made with the permission of the court but not otherwise;

- the court may not dispose of the application without a hearing; and
- the application notice must contain a prominent notice stating the possible consequences of the court making a committal order and of the respondent not attending the hearing: CPR PD 81, para.13.2.

Annex 3 to the PD provides for a form of warning to be included on committal applications:

> *"IMPORTANT NOTICE*
>
> *The Court has power to send you to prison, to fine you or seize your assets if it finds that any of the allegations made against you are true and amount to a contempt of court.* ***You must attend court*** *on the date shown on the front of this form. It is in your own interest to do so. You should bring with you any witnesses and documents which you think will help you put your side of the case. If you consider the allegations are not true you must tell the court why. If it is established that they are true, you must tell the court of any good reason why they do not amount to a contempt of court, or, if they do, why you should not be punished. If you need advice, you should show this document at once to your solicitor or go to a Citizens' Advice Bureau or similar organisation."*

Evidence in support

Written evidence in support of or in opposition to a committal application must be given by affidavit and filed with the court: CPR PD 81, paras.14.1 and 14.2. This does not prevent a respondent from giving evidence orally at the hearing, which is his right: r.81.28(2).

Procedural defects

On application by the respondent or on its own initiative, the court may strike out a committal application if it appears to the court that:

- the application and the evidence served in support of it disclose no reasonable ground for alleging that the respondent is guilty of a contempt of court;
- the application is an abuse of the court's process or, if made in existing proceedings, is otherwise likely to obstruct the just disposal of those proceedings; or
- there has been a failure to comply with a rule, practice direction or court order: CPR PD 81, para.16.1.

The court may waive any procedural defect in the commencement or conduct of a committal application if satisfied that no injustice has been caused to the respondent by the defect: CPR PD 81, para.16.2; and see *Nicholls v. Nicholls* [1997] 1 WLR 314.

A committal application may not be discontinued without the permission of the court: CPR PD 81, para.16.3.

Hearing

In the county court, a committal application should be heard by a Circuit Judge unless a statute provides otherwise (which, in the context of unlawful eviction and harassment, it does not) or a District Judge has been granted the power to do so by the Designated Circuit Judge of the County Court concerned: CPR PD 2B, paras.8.3, 11.1(d) and 14.1.

When issuing or filing the claim form or application notice for a committal application, the applicant must obtain from the court a date for the hearing of the committal application: CPR PD 81, para.15.1. This date must not be less than 14 days after service of the claim form or application notice on the respondent and must be specified in the claim form, application notice or a separate order served with those documents: CPR PD 81, para.15.2.

At the first hearing of the application, the court can adjourn it with case management directions where appropriate or, if the matter is ready to be heard (ordinarily only where the respondent admits the breach alleged) the court can proceed to determine the application: CPR PD PD, para.15.4.

Respondent's right to respond and obtain legal representation

A respondent must be given an opportunity to respond to the allegations and a reasonable time to do so (taking legal advice if desired) as well as the possibility of being able to obtain legal aid and how to contact the Legal Aid Agency and, if unable to understand English, allowed to make arrangements for an interpreter to attend the hearing: CPR PD 81, paras.15.5 and 15.6.

In *Brown v Haringey LBC* [2015] EWCA Civ 483, [2015] HLR 30, the Court of Appeal made clear that if a respondent is unrepresented then, save in circumstances of extreme urgency, an adjournment should be granted so that representation may be obtained. Bad behaviour earlier in the proceedings, including a tendency towards extreme truculence, is unlikely to justify proceeding without permitting the respondent to secure legal representation.

The relevant principles were summarised in *Egeneonu v Egeneonu* [2017] EWHC 2451 (Fam) and the specific point made that the more serious a case, the more a respondent is likely to need persuasive and skilful representation. "It is almost impossible to envisage a case where such representation will not be needed, if only to remind a judge of the principles which apply. Even in a case where a respondent admits each and every allegation alleged, representation will be needed so as to assist the judge in considering the appropriate disposal."

It is for now beyond doubt that non-means tested legal aid is available to defend committal proceedings: *All England Lawn Tennis Club (Championships) Ltd v McKay* [2019] EWHC 3065 (QB); [2020] 1 W.L.R. 216. In *Re O (Committal: Legal Representation)* [2019] EWCA Civ 1721, [2019] 4 W.L.R. 140, where legal representation had clearly been requested and wanted, it was held that alleged contemnors were entitled to be provided with legal representation "if they want it" and that they would qualify for non-means-tested legal aid.

See also by way of contrast the decision of *Fort Locks Self Storage Ltd v Deakin* [2017] EWCA Civ 1683 as to how far the obligation may extend (i.e. so as to affect the overall fairness of the procedure) and the recent decision in *Corrigan v Chelsea Football Club Ltd* [2019] EWCA Civ 1964; [2019] Costs L.R. 2097 where a ticket tout was found to have refused to engage with the proceedings and ignored repeated warnings. There were no indications that he had truly wanted legal representation, or that he had been prepared to take serious steps to obtain it.

Final hearing

At the final hearing of a committal application, the applicant is confined to the grounds on which the committal application was brought: CPR r.81.28(1).

The respondent is entitled to give oral evidence, whether or not he has filed or served written evidence, and, if doing so, may be cross-examined but can only call another witness with the permission of the court (whether or not they have provided affidavit evidence): CPR r.81.28(2).

The court can require any party or another person to give oral evidence at a committal hearing: CPR r.81.28(3).

If the respondent does not attend the hearing, the court can make a committal order in his absence and may fix a date and time when the respondent is to be brought before the court: CPR r.81.28(6). The factors for the court to consider when deciding whether to proceed in the defendant's absence include:

- Whether the respondents have been served with the relevant documents, including the notice of this hearing;

- Whether the respondents have had sufficient notice to enable them to prepare for the hearing;

- Whether any reason has been advanced for their non-appearance;
- Whether by reference to the nature and circumstances of the respondents' behaviour, they have waived their right to be present (i.e. is it reasonable to conclude that the respondents knew of, or were indifferent to, the consequences of the case proceeding in their absence);
- Whether an adjournment for would be likely to secure the attendance of the respondents, or at least facilitate their representation;
- The extent of the disadvantage to the respondents in not being able to present their account of events;
- Whether undue prejudice would be caused to the applicant by any delay;
- Whether undue prejudice would be caused to the forensic process if the application was to proceed in the absence of the respondents;
- The terms of the *'overriding objective'*, including the obligation on the court to deal with the case 'justly', including doing so *"expeditiously and fairly"*, and taking *"any … step or make any… order for the purposes of … furthering the overriding objective"*: *Sanchez v Oboz* [2015] EWHC 235 (Fam).

Powers of the court

On a committal application, the court can make a committal order which sends the contemnor to prison immediately or it can make a suspended order subject to conditions: CPR r.81.29. At the same time the committal order is made, a warrant of committal may be issued: CPR r.81.30.

The court can discharge a person in custody on application by the contemnor if they have purged, or which to purge, their contempt: CPR r.81.31.

Sentencing

On a finding of contempt, a contemnor is liable to a term of imprisonment for up to 2 years: s.14, Contempt of Court Act 1981. What sentence is imposed is entirely at the discretion of the court: *Longhurst Homes Ltd v Killen* [2008] EWCA Civ 402.

Ordinarily it will not be in the interests of a claimant to press for a fine (which can be unlimited) or sequestration of assets because this approach risks depleting the source of damages and/or costs in any ongoing claim.

First breaches tend to result in *suspended* prison sentences but, as is clear from the decision in *Saxby v McKinley* (1997) 29 H.L.R. 569, which concerned an injunction for reinstatement, a landlord is at risk of an immediate custodial sentence from the outset given the consequences to an occupant of being kept out of possession. In that case, the landlord was sentenced to an immediate custodial sentence of 28 days which the Court of Appeal upheld on appeal.

A Defendant will be released from custody upon serving half of a period of imprisonment: s.258 Criminal Justice Act 2003.

Appeals

The general rule is that an unsuccessful party to litigation requires permission to appeal against an order. However, by CPR r.52.3(1)(a)(i), that requirement is disapplied in the case of a committal order.

If a Circuit Judge makes a committal order in contempt proceedings the effect of which would be to deprive the contemnor of his liberty, then no permission is required to appeal to a single judge of the High Court against that order: see CPR PD 52A, Part II.

If a judge makes any other form of order in contempt proceedings (e.g. an order fining the contemnor or that the defendant pay the claimant's costs), that is not a "committal order" within the meaning of CPR r.52.3(1)(a) and permission to appeal is required: *Masri v Consolidated Contractors International Co SAL* [2011] EWCA Civ 898; [2011] C.P. Rep. 44; *Government of Sierra Leone v Davenport* [2002] EWCA Civ 230 and *Barnet LBC v Hurst* [2002] EWCA Civ 1009 at [25]-[27]; [2003] 1 WLR 722.

Despite the clear wording, the Court of Appeal has held that *only* the contemnor is exempt from the requirement to seek permission to appeal. The applicant still requires permission to appeal, whether against a dismissal of the application or against the sentence: *Barnet LBC v Hurst* [2002] EWCA Civ 1009; [2003] 1 WLR 722; *Kynaston v Carroll* [2004] EWCA Civ 1434; *Poole Borough Council v Hambridge* [2007] EWCA Civ 990. Permission to appeal is also required if the proposed appeal is a second appeal to the Court of Appeal.

POINTS OF NOTE

- **If personal service is likely to be difficult, efforts should be made to obtain provision in the order for an alternative method to be used such as "this order shall be sufficiently served for the purposes of any application to commit if it is read to him in full by telephone by midnight on [date]". A statement or certificate of service explaining precisely how this service was carried out should be produced.**

- **Before anything else, a claimant contemplating applying for committal of a defendant should check that the alleged breaches do in fact fall within the scope of the injunction, that the injunction order contained a penal notice and that it was properly served. A respondent should take the same course with a view to discouraging such an application or striking it out if made.**

- The provisions of Part 81 should be scrutinised carefully when making the application and providing evidence. Likewise, those advising respondents should look for procedural breaches.

- Respondents must be given the opportunity to obtain an interpreter where needed and legal aid in any case.

- If an undertaking is given, it must be complied with to the letter. Where an act must occur within a specified time, time is of the essence.

- A breach of an injunction or undertaking can result in a term of imprisonment for up to two years. A first breach can result in an immediate custodial sentence in the context of unlawful eviction because of the importance of a person being able to return to their home.

- Those advising a defendant who is accused of contempt should always have in mind the ability to apply to court to purge the contempt. In some cases, such an application can effectively avert a sentence of imprisonment.

CHAPTER NINE
FUNDING (CFAS, DBAS AND LEGAL AID)

This chapter looks in broad terms at the current approach to funding civil claims for unlawful eviction and/or harassment via the use of conditional fee agreements ("CFAs"), and damages-based agreements ("DBAs") which might be an option for clients wishing to fund such litigation. It also considers whether legal aid would be available.

FUNDING CIVIL CLAIMS

In 2009, the then Master of the Rolls tasked Lord Justice Rupert Jackson with reviewing the way in which costs in civil litigation operated and their impact on access to justice. One of the key concerns was the way in which conditional fee agreements ("CFAs") appeared to have a disproportionate impact on the costs payable by unsuccessful defendants in litigation such that it hindered access to justice. The outcome of that review was Jackson LJ's final report, presented to the Master of the Rolls on 14.1.10. The proposed reforms prompted a Government consultation in November 2010 which culminated, so far as relevant, in Part 2 of the Legal Aid, Sentencing and Punishment of Offenders Act 2012. As a result, in April 2013, there was a monumental shift in terms of the way in which CFAs operated.

Conditional fee agreements

The starting point is that claims *inter alia* for personal injury are dealt with in a different way to claims for other general damages.[1] A claim for unlawful eviction will generally not include a separate claim for personal injury because (i) such a claim can have a negative impact on the limi-

1 The main difference being that a PI claimant benefits from the principle of Qualified One-way Costs Shifting or "QOCS" whereby, in summary, an unsuccessful claimant does not pay the defendant's costs unless they fail to beat a Part 36 offer.

tation period for bringing claims; and (ii) much of the distress caused by an eviction (or harassment) is covered by a claim for distress and inconvenience. There may be some cases where a personal injury claim is appropriate, e.g. where there is clear evidence of physical or mental injury resulting from the eviction/harassment, for example an assault during the course of the eviction, an inability to access medication which results in a diabetic seizure, or post-traumatic stress disorder. However, such claims tend to be less common and in the main are reliant on a period of time having passed between the act(s) concerned and the manifestation of the physical injury. This chapter therefore examines the funding arrangements in place for what one might call a "conventional" claim for unlawful eviction and/or harassment and leaves to one side the regime applicable to personal injury claims.

What is a conditional fee agreement?

A conditional fee agreement is colloquially (and sometimes erroneously) referred to as a "no-win, no-fee" agreement. In general terms, it is a contract pursuant to which a solicitor agrees to represent a client in proceedings at no cost (or significantly reduced cost) to that client if the case is lost and where, if the case is won, the other side would be expected to pay the winning party's legal costs.

In practical terms, under a CFA, where a claimant loses a claim and is liable to pay e.g. his own disbursements (broadly costs payable to a third party such as experts and court fees) and the costs of the winning party, these costs are met by insurance (whether taken out before the event "BTE", as with car or home insurance for example, or after the event "ATE").

Prior to the commencement of s.58, Courts and Legal Services Act 1990 ("CLSA 1990"), such agreements were contrary to public policy as champertous[2] and were therefore unlawful at common law: *Hollins v Russell* [2003] EWCA Civ 718; [2003] 1 W.L.R. 2487, per Brooke LJ at [1].

2 Essentially the maintenance by a third party of litigation on the understanding he will share in the proceeds of it.

By s.58, CLSA 1990, Parliament first permitted CFAs in relation to the provision of advocacy or litigation services in certain narrowly prescribed circumstances. The section was brought into force in July 1993 and regulations governing the lawful use of CFAs followed in 1995: see Conditional Fee Agreements Order 1995 (SI 1995/1674) and the Conditional Fee Agreements Regulations 1995 (SI 1995/1675) now repealed and replaced (see below). When the scope of legal aid was significantly reduced in 2001, the use of CFAs was promoted as an alternative means of securing access to justice, but this drive had "unintended consequences".

Two aspects of the use of CFAs which prompted reform between 2009 and 2013 were the "success fee" and the ATE insurance premium. The former is a percentage uplift on the costs actually incurred by the CFA-funded litigant to reflect the risk to the solicitors in taking on the litigation and could be (and often was) as high as 100% of the costs actually incurred. This was payable to a CFA-funded party by the losing party. At the same time, where ATE insurance was taken out on a deferred and self-funded basis, the premium could be as high as 90% of the sum insured. The result was that an unsuccessful defendant was paying around four-times the amount of the value of the legal services provided to the opposing party: namely, his own legal costs, his opponent's base legal costs, the success fee of up to 100% and the ATE premium of up to 90%: see generally Jackson LJ's Final Report at Chapters 9 and 10.

The above prompted Jackson LJ to recommend that success fees and ATE insurance premiums be paid by the claimant rather than the defendant and that, to guard against the risk of an adverse costs order in the event the claimant lost, that the defendant be prevented from passing on its legal costs to the claimant. These recommendations were accepted and ultimately enacted by Part 2, LASPOA 2012 which came into force on 1.4.13.

How do CFAs operate in the context of an unlawful eviction/harassment claim?

Section 58(2), CLSA 1990 (as amended by s.44 of LASPOA 2012) states that a CFA is an agreement with a person providing advocacy or litigation services which provides for his fees and expenses, or any part of them, to be payable only in specified circumstances. For these purposes, a CFA provides for a success fee if it provides for the amount of any fees to which it applies to be increased, in specified circumstances, above the amount which would be payable if it were not payable only in specified circumstances (with the increase being referred to as the "success fee"). In summary therefore, a CFA is an agreement to pay for legal services where the amount paid for those services varies according to certain outcomes.

Where a CFA provides for a success fee (in claims not involving a claim for personal injury where other requirements come into play), certain conditions apply which are set out in s.58(3) to (4), CLSA 1990, namely:

- it must be in writing;
- it must not relate to proceedings which cannot be the subject of an enforceable conditional fee agreement (i.e., criminal proceedings, proceedings under s.82, Environmental Protection Act 1990 and family proceedings as defined – s.58A, CLSA 1990); and
- it must comply with such requirements (if any) as may be prescribed by the Lord Chancellor;
- it must relate to proceedings of a description specified by order made by the Lord Chancellor (being all proceedings save for those excluded under s.58 and proceedings under s.82, Environmental Protection Act 1990 – art.1, Conditional Fee Agreements Order 2013/689);

- it must state the percentage by which the amount of the fees which would be payable if it were not a conditional fee agreement is to be increased; and

- that percentage must not exceed the percentage specified in relation to the description of proceedings to which the agreement relates by order made by the Lord Chancellor (i.e. 100% - art.2, Conditional Fee Agreements Order 2013/689).

There are additional provisions (s.58(4A) and (4B)) not relevant here, which since 6 April 2019 apply to publication and privacy claims.

Section 58A, CLSA 1990 contains a number of supplementary provisions to s.58: in the definitions of "advocacy services" and "litigation services" as they apply for their purposes, "proceedings" includes any sort of proceedings for resolving disputes (and not just proceedings in a court), whether commenced or contemplated: s.58A(4), CLSA 1990; and a costs order made in proceedings may not include provision requiring the payment by one party of all or part of a success fee payable by another party under a conditional fee agreement: s.58A(6), CLSA 1990.

In unlawful eviction/harassment claims issued after 1.4.13, success fees and ATE insurance premiums are paid by the CFA-funded client, not the defendant as was previously the case.

Civil procedure rules

Rules of court may make provision with respect to the assessment of any costs which include fees payable under a conditional fee agreement (including one which provides for a success fee)": s.58A(7), CLSA 1990.

Prior to LASPOA 2012, the CPR provided that litigants who funded a claim by a CFA had obligations to notify the court and the other side of the funding arrangement (as the other side would potentially have to pay the success fee and ATE insurance premiums): CPR r.44.15(1).

Since LASPOA 2012,[3] the requirement to notify has been removed save in excepted cases (not relevant here) and for pre-commencement funding arrangements (highly unlikely to be relevant here).

CPR r.44.1(3) provides that where advocacy or litigation services are provided to a client under a conditional fee agreement, costs are recoverable under CPR Parts 44 to 47 notwithstanding that the client is liable to pay the legal representative's fees and expenses only to the extent that sums are recovered in respect of the proceedings, whether by way of costs or otherwise. The effect of this rule is to mitigate what is known as the "indemnity principle". Costs between parties are awarded as an *indemnity* to the party incurring them and a successful party cannot therefore recover a sum in excess of their liability to their own solicitor (*Gundry v Sainsbury* [1910] 1 K.B. 645). The indemnity principle creates an anomaly in the case of CFAs because the amount of costs for which a litigant is liable to pay his solicitor varies according to outcome and can be as little as nil if no costs order is obtained from the other side. To account for this, s.51, Senior Courts Act 1981 (as amended by s.31, Access to Justice Act 1999) provides for rules of court that permit the disapplication of the indemnity principle in the context of CFAs. That is what r.44.1(3) achieves. Costs assessment principles contained in CPR Parts 44-47 thus apply to CFA and non-CFA funded litigation.

CPR r.46.9(4) and PD 46, para.46.6.4 concern the assessment of costs between solicitor and client in the context of a CFA.

ATE insurance

It is often the case that when a party enters into a CFA, they will look to protect themselves for liability for the other side's costs if they lose the claim. This is commonly done by means of after the event ("ATE") insurance.

---

3 Save pre-commencement funding arrangement (i.e. broadly entered into prior to 1 April 2012).

By s.58C, CLSA 1990 (as inserted by s.46, LASPOA 2012), a costs order made in favour of a party to proceedings who has taken out a costs insurance policy may not include provision requiring the payment of an amount in respect of all or part of the premium of the policy, unless such provision is permitted by regulations. For these purposes, "costs insurance policy", means a policy insuring against the risk of the party incurring a liability in those proceedings and "proceedings" includes any sort of proceedings for resolving disputes (and not just proceedings in court), whether commenced or contemplated: s.58C(5), CLSA 1990.

By the Recovery of Costs Insurance Premiums in Clinical Negligence Proceedings (No. 2) Regulations 2013/739, reg.3, the only claims in which a costs order in proceedings can require payment of an amount of the premium are clinical negligence claims. As such, in unlawful eviction and harassment claims, the ATE premium must be borne by the insured party.

Section 46, LASPOA 2012 also repealed (subject to transitional cases) s.29, Access to Justice Act 1999, i.e., the provision for recovery of ATE insurance premiums from the other side.

Damages-based agreements

Damages-based agreements were originally confined to employment claims and permitted contingency fee agreements whereby the legal representative was paid out of the damages recovered: s.58AA, CLSA 1990.[4] LASPOA 2012, s.45 amended s.58AA, CLSA 1990 to remove the restriction of their use save in employment claims. As such, from 1.4.13, DBAs were available in all contentious business save family and criminal proceedings. Thus, by s.58AA(3), CLSA 1990 (as amended), a DBA is an agreement between a person providing advocacy services, litigation services or claims management services and the recipient of those services which provides that

4 Inserted by s.154, Coroners and Justice Act 2009 with effect from November 12, 2009 (s.182(1)(e), 2009 Act).

a) the recipient is to make a payment to the person providing the services if the recipient obtains a specified financial benefit in connection with the matter in relation to which the services are provided, and

b) the amount of that payment is to be determined by reference to the amount of the financial benefit obtained.

By s.58AA(4), CLSA 1990 such an agreement

- must be in writing;
- must not relate to proceedings which cannot be the subject of an enforceable CFA or to proceedings of a description prescribed by the Lord Chancellor (see above);
- must not provide for a payment above a prescribed amount or for a payment above an amount calculated in a prescribed manner. In this respect, reg.4 of the Damages-based Agreement Regulations 2013/609 provides that
    - a DBA must not require an amount to be paid by the client other than:
        - the payment, net of

            i. any costs (including fixed costs under CPR Part 45); and

            ii. where relevant, any sum in respect of disbursements incurred by the representative in respect of counsel's fees,

          that have been paid or are payable by another party to the proceedings by agreement or order; and

        - any expenses incurred by the representative, net of any amount which has been paid or is payable by another party to the proceedings by agreement or order;

    - (in claims or proceedings at first instance only which do not involve a claim for personal injury) a DBA must not provide for a payment above an amount which, including VAT, is equal to 50% of the sums ultimately recovered by the client; and

- must comply with the requirements as to its terms and conditions as set out in reg.3 of the Damages-Based Agreements Regulations 2013/609 namely, and so far as relevant, that the terms and conditions of a DBA must specify

    - the claim or proceedings or parts of them to which the DBA relates;

    - the circumstances in which the representative's payment, expenses and costs, or part of them, are payable; and

    - the reason for setting the amount of the payment at the level agreed.

For these purposes, "payment" includes a transfer of assets and any other transfer of money's worth (and the reference above to "a payment above a prescribed amount, or above an amount calculated in a prescribed manner" is construed accordingly).

"Claims management services" are a particular form of legal advisory service and the meaning of the phrase in this context is the same as in Part 2 of the Compensation Act 2006 (see s.4(2) of that Act).

As is the case for CFAs, "proceedings" in context includes any sort of proceedings for resolving disputes (and not just proceedings in a court), whether commenced or contemplated: s.58AA(7A), CLSA 1990.

Civil procedure rules

As with CFAs, by s.58AA(6A), CLSA 1990, rules of court may make provision with respect to the assessment of costs in proceedings where a party in whose favour a costs order is made has entered into a DBA in connection with the proceedings.

CPR r.44.18 provides that:

- the fact that a party has entered into a damages-based agreement will not affect the making of any order for costs which otherwise would be made in favour of that party;
- where costs are to be assessed in favour of a party who has entered into a damages-based agreement
    - the party's recoverable costs will be assessed in accordance with CPR r.44.3 (the general costs assessment principles which include proportionality); and
    - the party may not recover by way of costs more than the total amount payable by that party under the damages-based agreement for legal services provided under that agreement (i.e. the percentage plus disbursements and counsel's fees).

It is apparent from the above that the indemnity principle applies to DBAs. The effect is that costs recovery under a DBA is capped at the amount of the contingency fee and does not extend to all recoverable costs.

Reform of DBAs

There has been considerable negative publicity associated with the use of DBAs arising not only from the lack of clarity in the 2013 DBA Regulations but also from the appropriateness of recovering payment from damages (which bears closer relation to champerty than a CFA) and particularly whether they should be used at all where an alternative exists (such as CFAs). The general consensus appears to be to avoid them where possible. This attitude has been acknowledged recently by the Ministry of Justice. In the post-implementation review of Part 2, LASPOA 2012, published on 7 February 2019, two areas of concern were identified, one of which was the need for clarity and certainty in the use of DBAs. The majority of respondents had found the regulations ineffective and all respondents had called for their reform and redrafting.

In December 2018, the MOJ arranged for the 2013 DBA Regulations to be redrafted. The proposed draft SI (Damages-based Agreements Regulations 2019) can be found at https://www.qmul.ac.uk/law/media/law/docs/research/DBA-Regs-2019-(NB-and-RM,-13-Oct-2019),-20.30.pdf. The draft regulations include significant operational changes to reflect the new approach and should be considered in detail.

In summary, the draft 2019 Regulations will apply to any new contentious business save family, criminal and employment matters (the latter of which will remain subject to the 2013 Regulations). The model for DBAs has been abandoned: rather than recoverable costs effectively being set off against the capped proportion of damages recovered ("the DPA payment") under what is known as the "Ontario model" (see reg.4, 2013 DBA Regulations, above), the new regulations use a "success fee model" where, on receipt of a financial benefit (as more broadly defined to reflect the wording in s.58AA, CLSA 1990 and to include real or personal property or a chose in action), the party would pay his representative his recoverable costs and expenses (not including counsel's fees) separate to the DPA payment rather than them being incorporated within it. The DPA payment would include counsel's fees and any irrecoverable costs and/or VAT. This addresses the disincentive arising from the operation of the indemnity principle on DBAs. The percentage caps on costs recoverable from damages are reduced to ensure representatives are not overcompensated.

Additionally, there is provision for remuneration in the event of no financial benefit being recovered i.e. up to 30% of irrecoverable costs. One issue that arises in this context is what happens if the client is partially successful to a limited extent and does not recover his costs. The representative may be put in a position where he would be remunerated to a greater extent if the client lost outright.

This issue will no doubt be considered as part of the supplementary report, to be prepared in the light of feedback provided in November 2019. It is anticipated that this report will be made available in the second half of 2020.

Legal aid

At the same time that changes were implemented in relation to the availability of CFAs and DBAs to fund civil litigation, additional restrictions were put in place on when civil legal aid would be available in certain housing-related cases. The restrictions impacted particularly on disrepair claims where damages were the only remedy sought but, as is so often the case, the message as received by the public was that legal aid was no longer generally available for housing cases which, on its face, include claims for damages for unlawful eviction and/or harassment in a landlord and tenant context.

It is important to emphasise therefore the continuing availability of legal aid for claims for unlawful eviction.

By s.9, LASPOA 2012, civil legal services are to be available to an individual under Part 2 if:

a) they are civil legal services described in Part 1 of Schedule 1, and

b) the Director has determined that the individual qualifies for the services in accordance with this Part (and has not withdrawn the determination).

So far as relevant, para.33 of Sch.1, LASPOA 2012 provides:

"33 Loss of home

(1) Civil legal services provided to an individual in relation to—

(a) court orders for sale or possession of the individual's home, or

(b) the eviction from the individual's home of the individual or others.

[…]

General exclusions

(3) Sub-paragraphs (1) and (2) are subject to the exclusions in Part 2 of this Schedule, with the exception of paragraph 14 of that Part.

(4) But the exclusions described in sub-paragraph (3) are subject to the exceptions in sub-paragraphs (5) and (6).

[…]

(6) The services described in sub-paragraph (1) include services described in any of paragraphs 3 to 6 or 8 of Part 2 of this Schedule to the extent that they are—

(a) […]

(b) services provided to an individual in relation to the unlawful eviction from the individual's home of the individual or others.

(7) Sub-paragraphs (1) and (2) are subject to the exclusion in Part 3 of this Schedule.

[…]

Definitions

(9) In this paragraph "home", in relation to an individual, means the house, caravan, houseboat or other vehicle or structure that is the individual's only or main residence, subject to sub-paragraph (10).

(10) References in this paragraph to an individual's home do not include a vehicle or structure occupied by the individual if—

(a) there are no grounds on which it can be argued that the individual is occupying the vehicle or structure otherwise than as a trespasser, and

(b) there are no grounds on which it can be argued that the individual's occupation of the vehicle or structure began otherwise than as a trespasser.

(11) In sub-paragraphs (9) and (10), the references to a caravan, houseboat or other vehicle include the land on which it is located or to which it is moored.

(12) For the purposes of sub-paragraph (10) individuals occupying, or beginning occupation, of a vehicle or structure as a trespasser include individuals who do so by virtue of—

(a) title derived from a trespasser, or

(b) a licence or consent given by a trespasser or a person deriving title from a trespasser.

(13) For the purposes of sub-paragraph (10) an individual who is occupying a vehicle or structure as a trespasser does not cease to be a trespasser by virtue of being allowed time to leave the vehicle or structure."

Unlawful eviction

Schedule 1, para.33, LASPOA 2012 permits legal aid to be granted to an individual for the provision of civil legal services in relation to eviction from the home whether alone or with others (and so would include family members or friends so far as a cause of action could be established). The use of the phrase "in relation to" suggests this provision is to be construed broadly and would certainly encompass an injunction claim as well as a freestanding claim for damages for unlawful eviction (as shown by the subsequent reference to unlawful eviction in sub-para.(6), and probably injunction/damages claims for acts conducted with a view to unlawfully evicting an individual (such as harassment likely to cause a person to cease occupation of his home).

That starting point is qualified to an extent by Sch.1, Part 2, LASPOA 2012 which excludes certain services from being provided to recipients of civil legal aid most notably in relation to claims for personal injury (para.1), for the torts of assault and battery (para.3), for trespass to goods or land (paras.4 and 5), for damage to property (para.6) and for breach of statutory duty (para.8). Claims for breach of contract are not excluded under Part 2.

However, as can be seen from Sch.1, para.33(4), some of the exclusions in Sch.1, Part 2, LASPOA 2012 are disapplied so far as prescribed by para.33(6) in relation to a claim for unlawful eviction, specifically Sch.1, Part 2, paras.3-6 and 8. Consequently, legal aid is available in relation to civil claims based on most of the causes of action relevant to unlawful eviction.

Protection from harassment

There is separate provision within Schedule 1 of LASPOA 2012 dealing with protection from harassment, namely para.37 which provides that, subject to the usual qualifying conditions, legal aid will be available for:

> *"(1) Civil legal services provided in relation to—*
>
> > *(a) an injunction under section 3 or 3A of the Protection from Harassment Act 1997;*
> >
> > *(b) the variation or discharge of a restraining order under section 5 or 5A of that Act.*
>
> *Exclusions*
>
> *(2) Sub-paragraph (1) is subject to the exclusions in Parts 2 and 3 of this Schedule."*

It should be noted that whilst para.8 of Part 2 excludes civil legal services provided in relation to a claim in tort in respect of breach of statutory duty, any claim for an injunction under ss.3 or 3A, PHA 1997 is a standalone remedy and not contingent on bringing a claim *in tort* for breach of those duties.

It would seem however that if the only basis on which a claim for harassment were brought was under PHA 1997, then legal aid would not be available for any damages claim.

The "Check if you can get legal aid" service on the GOV.UK website also confirm that legal aid is available to those facing eviction and whose landlord is harassing them (subject to financial eligibility).

<u>Eligibility</u>

Having identified that the claim for unlawful eviction and harassment (so far as it relates to enjoyment of the home which in this context it almost certainly will) is within scope, to be eligible for legal aid, the claimant will have to show that:

- he does not have access to other potential sources of funding (other than a conditional fee agreement) from which it would be reasonable to fund the case;
- the case is unsuitable for a conditional fee agreement;
- there is no person other than the individual, including a person who might benefit from the proceedings, who can reasonably be expected to bring the proceedings
- the individual has exhausted all reasonable alternatives to bringing proceedings including any complaints system, ombudsman scheme or other form of alternative dispute resolution;

- there is a need for representation in all the circumstances of the case including,
  - the nature and complexity of the issues;
  - the existence of other proceedings; and
  - the interests of other parties to the proceedings; and
- the proceedings are not likely to be allocated to the small claims track (which they cannot be in a claim for unlawful eviction);
- the claim has prospects of success which are moderate (50-60%), good (60-80%) or very good (80%+) (and where borderline and the case is of significant wider public interest; or a case with overwhelming importance to the individual);
- the taking of proceedings is proportionate, having regard to the benefit to the claimant, the likely costs and all the circumstances of the case; and
- the landlord or other person responsible for the matter complained of has been notified of the individual's complaint (except where this is impracticable) and, where such notice has been given, the landlord or other person has had a reasonable opportunity to resolve the matter

  – Civil Legal Aid (Merits Criteria) Regulations 2013 SI No 104, regs 39, 41, 43 and 62 and Lord Chancellor's Guidance under s.4.

POINTS TO NOTE

- **The use of CFAs and DBAs might be of benefit to a claimant or defendant in an unlawful eviction and harassment claim but advisors should be very clear as to the appropriateness of** their use if the claim is likely to turn on the credibility of the parties as assessed at court (e.g. where a respondent contends a person occupied under an excluded category of occupation).

- Practitioners should keep a close eye on developments relating to the use of DBAs.

- Legal aid is *prima facie* available for injunction and/or damages claims for unlawful eviction but only for injunctions under the PHA 1997 for harassment.

- Even if the claim falls within scope, the claimant will have to show that he is eligible for assistance, applying *inter alia* the merits and proportionality criteria and ensuring the landlord has had notice of the claimant's complaint unless not practicable to do so.

CHAPTER TEN
BRINGING A CLAIM FOR UNLAWFUL EVICTION AND HARASSMENT

This chapter will look in practical terms at how a claim for unlawful eviction and harassment is brought and managed through to trial. The reality is that most claims for unlawful eviction are unlikely to cross the threshold for commencement in the High Court (where a claim should ordinarily be issued if its value is in excess of £100,000: CPR, 7APD.2 at 2.2). As such, this chapter focuses on procedure as it would apply in a County Court claim.

The process in outline is:

1. taking instructions from the client;
2. complying with the Practice Direction on pre-action conduct where possible;
3. considering whether an urgent injunction for reinstatement and/or delivery up of property is required (whether on notice or not) and making that application where appropriate (see Chapter 7);
4. drafting the claim, injunction application and witness statement;
5. obtaining or resisting interim remedies;
6. responding to the claim;
7. compliance with directions (including the preparation of evidence for trial); and

8. the trial (including where costs should fall – at all stages, the client should be protecting their position on costs).

PRE-ACTION

It is assumed for present purposes that attempts to resolve an unlawful eviction, harassment or related conduct short of litigation (e.g. by contacting the local authority for the area in which the accommodation is situated) are inappropriate in the circumstances or have proved unsuccessful.

It is also assumed that the client is in a position to fund the litigation whether pursuant to a conditional fee agreement or under legal aid (see Chapter 9).

Taking instructions from the client

It is imperative that those acting for occupants who have been unlawfully evicted and/or harassed (referred to here as "claimants") or for those accused of evicting them ("defendants") have clear and complete instructions as to the following matters (which are not exclusive) before embarking on advising as to what civil remedies may be available:

- A description of the premises from which the claimant is said to have been evicted: not only the address but the layout (this may become relevant e.g. if it is contended that any tenancy or licence was shared or that no permission to occupy was ever given or was revoked as a result of changes in occupancy and location of that occupancy).

- A contact number for the defendant to enable an immediate request for reinstatement to be made where appropriate.

- The names and addresses for service of the parties – the landlord's address for service will be his last known address whether provided pursuant to s.47/48, Landlord and Tenant

Act 1987 (in the case of a claim brought by a residential tenant) or ascertained from the Land Registry.

- The occupation status of the claimant immediately prior to their eviction – were they a tenant, a licensee or something else?
- Who occupied the premises with them immediately prior to the eviction?
- The factual circumstances of the eviction and any conduct which occurred prior to it which amounted to harassment in as much detail as possible including whether police attended and if so whether the parties' details were taken and a crime reference number obtained. Details of potential witnesses should be obtained including from any hotel which provided accommodation, any local authority officer if contacted, family members or neighbours.
- Was the defendant warned about the repercussions of his conduct prior to the eviction by e.g. the claimant, police or local authority officer? This will go to the "deliberateness" of the conduct which will impact on damages (particularly any aggravating or punitive element).
- What happened to the claimant's belongings if anything and can they be returned? If not, what was their market value at the time they were taken and what evidence can be obtained to support this (what are people paying for comparable items on e.g. Facebook Marketplace or Ebay)?
- Precisely what acts and/or omissions the claimant or defendant says have occurred and what effect those acts/omissions have had on them and/or members of their family (e.g. are they frightened, have they suffered from disturbed sleep, are they experiencing depressive symptoms, has it prevented the claimant from going to work as family members do not want to remain alone in the premises?)

- What if any defences are available to the alleged conduct (e.g. if the eviction is admitted, why did it happen and what was the defendant's belief at the time)?

Once detailed instructions have been taken, an advisor should consider if the claim has merit and if so, whether the client is best advised to seek (i) injunctive relief for any harassment or threats of eviction and, (ii) in the event of an eviction, reinstatement, or to look for accommodation elsewhere if it has not already been obtained. If reinstatement is something the claimant wants then an advisor should consider whether contacting the defendant in the first instance is appropriate (if threats of violence have been made, it may be wholly inappropriate to make direct contact) or whether an application for an injunction requesting reinstatement (and return of belongings or a prohibition on harassment where appropriate) should be made.

As part of this process, clients should be warned of the effect that failing to seek reinstatement may have on the measure of damages available at trial (see *Smith v Khan*, in Chapters 4 and 6).

If reinstatement is not an appropriate or likely outcome then advisors should consider how best to secure alternative accommodation (by e.g. making an application as homeless to the local housing authority for the area in which the claimant is currently present under the homelessness provisions in Part VII, HA 1996).

Complying with the pre-action protocol where possible

There is no specific pre-action protocol relating to unlawful eviction and harassment claims. The pre-action protocol Practice Direction ("PD") provides at para.3:

> *"Before commencing proceedings, the court will expect the parties to have exchanged sufficient information to*
>
> *(a) understand each other's position;*
>
> *(b) make decisions about how to proceed;*

(c) try to settle the issues without proceedings;

(d) consider a form of Alternative Dispute Resolution (ADR) to assist with settlement;

(e) support the efficient management of those proceedings; and

(f) reduce the costs of resolving the dispute."

This should be complied with in a claim for unlawful eviction and harassment. The PD states that where there is no relevant pre-action protocol, the parties should exchange correspondence and information to comply with the objectives above, bearing in mind that compliance should be proportionate: PD, para.6.

The steps will *usually* include:

(a) the claimant writing to the defendant with concise details of the claim. The letter should include the basis on which the claim is made, a summary of the facts, what the claimant wants from the defendant, and if money, how the amount is calculated;

(b) the defendant responding within a reasonable time - 14 days in a straight-forward case and no more than 3 months in a very complex one. The reply should include confirmation as to whether the claim is accepted and, if it is not accepted, the reasons why, together with an explanation as to which facts and parts of the claim are disputed and whether the defendant is making a counterclaim as well as providing details of any counterclaim; and

(c) the parties disclosing key documents relevant to the issues in dispute: PD, para.6.

The PD encourages the parties to consider negotiation or some other form of ADR (mediation, arbitration or early neutral evaluation) with a view to settling the proceedings without the need to issue a claim at all and, if a claim is issued, to resolving it thereafter: PD, para.9. Information on mediation and other forms of ADR is available in the Jackson ADR Handbook (available from Oxford University Press) or at https://civilmediation.org/for-the-public/about-mediation/ – (correct as at 15.6.20).

The parties should carry out a review of their respective positions: PD, para 12. The ideal time to carry out this review in a claim for unlawful eviction and harassment is prior to the commencement of the claim (or seeking interim relief if earlier) and (insofar as has not been an ongoing process) again after disclosure and inspection of documents and any expert report has been obtained.

It also warns of the fact that if a dispute proceeds to trial the court will look for evidence of compliance with the pre-action protocol: PD, para 13. This is often the part of a trial which is least prepared and can have significant costs implications. An advisor should keep a detailed record of correspondence and note for the purposes of instructing counsel or conveying to the court when key aspects of the protocol were complied with, when offers of settlement or mediation were made and what response was received. In the flurry of activity (and often settlement attempts) that take place shortly before trial, there is often inadequate time to fully grasp the *inter partes* correspondence.

That said, the court will consider whether all parties have complied *in substance* with the its terms and is not likely to be concerned with minor or technical infringements, especially when the matter is urgent (for example an application for an injunction): PD, para 15.

The consequences of non-compliance with the PD can be serious: PD, para 16. The court has a number of options available to it:

- relieving the parties of the obligation to comply or further comply with the PD;
- staying the claim while particular steps are taken to comply with the PD;

- applying sanctions including orders for costs (including indemnity costs), depriving a successful party of interest or awarding a lower rate of interest and, conversely, awarding a higher rate of interest (not exceeding 10%) on the judgment sum if the defaulting party is the defendant.

Limitation

Limitation periods must still be observed regardless of compliance with the PD: PD, para 17. If necessary, a protective claim form should be issued and the claim stayed pending compliance with the PD. Any negotiations in such circumstances would have to deal with the costs of issuing the claim (including any delay on the claimant's part such that it became necessary to issue protectively).

THE CLAIM

Urgent injunctions where appropriate

Alongside (or prior to) compliance with the PD, an application for an urgent injunction can be made. The law and procedure relating to injunctions has been discussed in Chapter 7.

Any application for an urgent injunction will ordinarily be made to the County Court for the area in which the claimant or defendant lives. The CPR PD 25A, para.4.2 directs that urgent applications and applications without notice (whether or not the claim has been issued) are normally dealt with at a court hearing but in cases of *extreme* urgency may be dealt with by telephone.

A landlord given no notice of an application for an injunction should ensure that on being served with the order of the court, they comply with it. The risk of failing to do so is imprisonment, a fine or sequestration of assets. Once the order is complied with, the landlord can consider whether to apply to discharge (or vary) the order or file evidence for the purposes of the return hearing in the hope the order is discharged or varied.

Defendants given short notice of applications should attempt to attend the hearing where possible or at least write to the claimant's legal representatives or directly to court making representations as to why the injunction ought not be made (and attaching any relevant documents where possible). The duty of full and frank disclosure would require such correspondence to be brought to the court's attention in any event but the correspondence should be clear that this is what the landlord wants the claimant to do.

Obtaining urgent or without notice interim remedies – obligations

The conduct of an urgent or without notice application for an injunction is dealt with in Chapter 7 on injunctions, including the duty of full and frank disclosure and the need to provide witness statements regarding any evidence given to the court via submissions after the event.

If an order is obtained without notice, it must either be served personally on the defendant or provision for alternative method of service obtained and its contents (including the penal notice) communicated to the defendant in accordance with that alternative method (usually by telephone or email).

The claim, injunction application and witness statements in support

A Part 7 claim in the county court is commenced by filing a claim form (N1). Particulars of claim ordinarily accompany the claim form but, if not, can be served within 14 days and a copy provided to the court within 7 days thereafter. The fact the particulars of claim have not been served does not prevent an application for an injunction being made. Practitioners should follow the procedural rules for bringing claims in CPR Part 7.

A claim only for harassment, is commenced using claim form N208 and follows the Part 8 procedure (see Chapter 5) unless transferred to Part 7 by the court.

The defence

Upon being served with a claim form under Part 7, the defendant has the option of either filing and serving a defence within 14 days or of serving an acknowledgement of service and thereby extending the time in which the file and serve the defence to 28 days: CPR r.15.4(1). That deadline can be extended by agreement for up to 28 days and the defendant must notify the court of any such agreement in writing: CPR r.15.5. The defendant can file and serve a counterclaim with his defence without the court's permission. If he does not do so but later wishes to counterclaim, the court's permission is required: CPR rr.15.7 and 20.4(2).

If only a claim for harassment is brought, the defendant must file and serve an acknowledgement of service and comply with the requirements of CPR Part 8 (see Chapter 5).

The reply

If the claimant wishes to reply to the defence (which course should not be uncommon in unlawful eviction and harassment claims where a defence is based on the status of the occupier and/or relates to a reasonably held belief), he must file it with a directions questionnaire and serve it on the other party at the same time: CPR r.15.8. The time limit for filing directions questionnaires in cases of unlawful eviction and harassment is 28 days from the date they are served by the court on the party: CPR r.26.3(1) and (6)(b)(ii).

The filing of a reply should ordinarily conclude the pleadings but there is scope for replying to a reply with the court's permission: CPR r.15.9.

Allocation of the claim

Upon a defence being filed, the court will provisionally decide to which track the claim should be allocated and give notice to the parties of that provisional decision and require them to file directions questionnaires by a specified date: CPR r.26.1.

A party may, when filing the completed directions questionnaire, make a written request for the proceedings to be stayed while the parties try to settle the case by alternative dispute resolution or other means: CPR r.26.4(1). If all parties request a stay the proceedings will be stayed for one month and the court will notify the parties accordingly: CPR r.26.4(2).

Claims for unlawful eviction will not be allocated to the small claims track: CPR r.26.7(4). Whether the claim is allocated to the fast track or the multi-track will depend on the factors in CPR r.26.8(1) including the financial value of the claim (the fast track being the usual track for claims for not more than £25,000 where the trial will last for not more than a day with expert evidence limited to not more than two fields and only one expert per field per party (r.26.4 and r.26.5)); the nature of the remedy sought; the likely complexity of the facts, law or evidence; and the amount of oral evidence which may be required.

Directions

Depending on to which track the claim is allocated, the court will set directions for the trial including (on the fast track) a timetable for disclosure of documents, service of witness statements and any expert evidence: CPR r.28.3, and (on the multi-track) such matters as are included in any relevant model directions: CPR r.29.1. The model standard directions for the multi-track can be found at https://www.justice.gov.uk/courts/procedure-rules/civil/standard-directions/general/list-of-cases-of-common-occurance.

Disclosure and inspection

A detailed exposition of the law and rules relating to disclosure and inspection are beyond the scope of this book. However, in broad terms, disclosure is the means by the court ensures all the parties' (and sometimes non-parties') cards are on the table. The duty is ongoing until judgment has been given or settlement.

On the fast track, it requires each party to disclose only documents: on which he relies; which adversely affect his own case or another party's case; which support another party's case; or which he is required to disclose by a relevant practice direction: CPR r.31.6. This type of disclosure obligation is referred to as "standard disclosure" and the procedure relating to it is set out in CPR r.31.10.

On the multi-track, standard disclosure is no longer the default position in claims not involving personal injury: CPR r.31.5(1) and (2). In such a claim, not less than 14 days before the first case management conference each party must file and serve a report verified by a statement of truth, which:

- describes briefly what documents exist or may exist that are or may be relevant to the matters in issue in the case;
- describes where and with whom those documents are or may be located;
- in the case of electronic documents, describes how those documents are stored;
- estimates the broad range of costs that could be involved in giving standard disclosure in the case, including the costs of searching for and disclosing any electronically stored documents; and
- states which of the directions under paragraphs (7) or (8) are to be sought: CPR r.31.5(3).

The parties must thereafter (not less than seven days before the first CMC) discuss and seek to agree a proposal for disclosure that meets the overriding objective: CPR r.31.5(5). If agreed, the court can approve them without a hearing and give directions in the terms proposed: CPR r.31.5(6). If not, at the first or any subsequent case management conference, the court will decide, having regard to the overriding objective and the need to limit disclosure to that which is necessary to deal with the case justly, what type of order for disclosure should be made under CPR r.31.5(7) and (8).

A party to whom a document is disclosed generally has a right to inspect it unless:

- The document is no longer in the control of the party who disclosed it. Control for these purposes means in the party's physical possession; where the party has a right to possession, and where the party has a right to inspect or take copies (e.g. pursuant to a request under the Data Protection Act 2018): CPR 31.8(2).

- The party disclosing the document has a right or a duty to withhold inspection of it (e.g. on grounds of privilege).

- A party considers that it would be disproportionate to the issues in the case to permit inspection of that document.

- CPR r.78.26 applies (where a person seeks disclosure or inspection of mediation evidence that is in the control of a mediator or mediation administrator): CPR r.31.3.

Practitioners should be aware that disclosure and inspection can be one of the difficult procedural steps to navigate in a claim. It is often used as a tactical springboard with attempts to delay or avoid disclosing or permitting inspection of documents. The parties should be astute to such tactics and prepared to make applications to the court for appropriate unless orders and sanctions.

Preparing evidence for trial

CPR Parts 32 and 33 and the PDs thereto govern the procedure and miscellaneous rules of evidence for trial.

The claimant's evidence will understandably be key and by the time the matter comes to trial, there may be several witness statements which have been produced (the first is often in support of or countering any application for interim relief and the remainder tend to provide more detail – in the light of disclosure – about the substantive claim).

It cannot be over-emphasised that in the post-Jackson era, the need for the parties to comply with directions is of paramount importance from both a reputational and costs perspective. Ultimately, both time and money can be wasted through satellite correspondence and litigation relating to whether automatic sanctions for failing to file costs budgets or witness statements in time apply. Written requests to extend time for exchange of witness statements for up to 28 days should be made as soon as an extension looks like it may be needed. Likewise, if longer than 28 days is needed, applications to extend time should be agreed swiftly and appropriate consent orders lodged with the court (and fees paid).

In terms of evidence, obvious examples which are likely to be relevant in many if not most cases include:

- Witness statements from those who can give evidence of the eviction or the surrounding circumstances;
- Tenancy agreements, licences, emails showing the basis of the occupation arrangement;
- Rent books where relevant;
- Bank statements showing payments made to the defendant in rent or otherwise;
- Police reports where relevant;
- Text messages/emails;
- Journal entries where relevant (or date and time-stamped posts on social media accounts referencing any incidents);
- Mobile phone video footage or CCTV of eviction;
- Receipts or bank statements showing purchases;

- Witness statements from family members who can attest to gifting belongings;
- photos of jewellery being worn/pictures/photos/wedding dresses/televisions/laptops etc. (check any relevant social media accounts for these photos);
- Expert GP evidence (not just letters which carry considerably less weight than a CPR compliant report); and
- Expert valuation evidence where s.28, HA 1988 damages are sought.

Expert on s.28 damages

CPR Part 35 governs the procedure relating to use of experts.

The pre-action protocol addresses the issue of expert evidence: at para.7. Many disputes can be resolved without expert advice or evidence. If it is necessary to obtain expert evidence, particularly in low value claims, the parties should consider using a single expert, jointly instructed by the parties, with the costs shared equally.

In claims for unlawful eviction and harassment, expert evidence is likely to be needed on two counts: first if s.27, HA 1988 is relied upon then it will need to show the difference in monetary value between the sale value of the premises with a sitting tenant and one without, referred to in s.28, HA 1988; secondly, it may be needed from a medical professional to support the effect of the eviction/harassment on the claimant in terms of deterioration in his physical or mental health or that of his family.

If such an expert is required, permission must be sought from the court at the first directions hearing: CPR r.35.4(1). In most claims, a single, jointly instructed expert for the purposes of valuation would be considered proportionate. If the evidence of the joint expert is clearly disadvantageous to either party, questions can be put in the first instance. If the responses are unhelpful, it is possible for the party to apply for a separate expert although the court will be mindful of the extent to which granting permission for such an expert is necessary and will impact on the overriding objective in CPR r.1: see e.g. *Daniels v Walker* [2000] 1 WLR 1382, CA.

TRIAL

The general rule is that trials are held in public: CPR r.39.2 and recorded: CPR r.39.9(1).

Unless the court orders otherwise, the claimant must file a trial bundle containing documents required by a relevant practice direction; and any court orders not more than 7 days and not less than 3 days before the start of the trial: CPR r.39.(5).

The trial will generally be preceded by skeleton arguments provided by the parties' legal representatives and a case summary and trial timetable.

The claimant will usually open the case, setting out the legal and factual issues for the court to determine. This process is often quite short if skeleton arguments have been provided. The claimant's evidence is heard first.

The general rule is that any fact which needs to be proved by the evidence of witnesses is proved at trial by their oral evidence given in public: CPR r.32.2(1). There are exceptions to this rule: those contained elsewhere in the CPR and if the court orders otherwise: CPR r.32.2(2). However, witnesses in civil litigation cannot simply turn up and provide their evidence (unless the court allows it); such evidence must first be provided by witness statement in accordance with directions: CPR r.32.4. If this is done, the witness' statement stands as his evidence in chief unless the court orders otherwise: CPR r.32.5(2). Importantly, the witness can (with the court's permission, it being satisfied that there is good reason not to confine the evidence of the witness to the contents of his witness statement) amplify on his witness statement and give any evidence of new matters which have arisen since the witness statement was served: CPR r.32.5(3) and (4).

After the claimant and his witnesses has been examined in-chief, the defendant has an opportunity to cross-examine the witness. This ordinarily takes the form of short, closed questions designed to illicit "yes" or "no" answers. It is an opportunity to test the witness' credibility and for the defendant to put his version of the facts to the claimant for comment. Once the claimant's evidence has been heard, the defendant presents his evidence and is cross-examined.

At the conclusion of the evidence, the parties give their closing speeches based on the evidence adduced in-chief and by cross-examination (the defendant first, followed by the claimant – who thereby gets the "last word"). Generally, the judge then takes time to consider his judgment and either gives that at the trial (ex tempore) or hands it down in writing at a later hearing.

After judgment is given, the parties generally make their submissions on costs.

COSTS

What follows is a brief overview of the approach the court takes when determining what costs orders should be made. For a detailed consideration of the area, see Cook on Costs 2020.

Generally

The court has discretion as to whether costs are payable by one party to another; the amount of those costs; and when they are to be paid: CPR r.44.2(1). If the court decides to make an order about costs, the general rule is that costs "follow the event" i.e., whoever wins is presumed to get his costs of the claim but the court may make any different order: CPR r.44.2(2).

In deciding what order (if any) to make about costs, the court will have regard to all the circumstances, including the conduct of all the parties (see also r.44.2(5)); whether a party has succeeded on part of its case, even if that party has not been wholly successful; and any admissible offer to settle made by a party which is drawn to the court's attention, and which is not an offer to which costs consequences under Part 36 apply: CPR r.44.2(4).

Where the court finds a party liable for the other side's costs in a fast track claim, it is encouraged to assess the costs of the whole claim at the trial: CPR PD 44, para.9.2. Otherwise the usual rule is that the costs go off for a detailed assessment. It is important that practitioners file and serve their statement of costs in good time or it risks the court refusing to make an order at all or ordering detailed assessment (which is more expensive, time-consuming and results in a delay to the client recovering all of the costs payable to him).

Where the court orders a party to pay costs subject to detailed assessment, it will order that party to pay a reasonable sum on account of costs, unless there is good reason not to do so: CPR r.44.2(8). Broadly, under CPR r.3.18, in a case where a costs budget has been approved or agreed, when assessing costs on the standard basis the court must have regard to that budget and not depart from it unless satisfied that there is good reason to do so. In *Cleveland Bridge UK LTD v Sarens (UK) Ltd* [2018] EWHC 827 (TCC); [2018] 2 Costs L.R. Joanna Smith QC held that the starting point was 90% of approved budgeted costs (although for costs incurred (which do not form part of an approved budget – see CPR PD 3E, para.7.4 and *MacInnes v Gross* [2017] EWHC 127 (QB); [2017] 2 Costs L.R. 243 *per* Davies LJ at [46]-[47]) the approach was to assess a reasonable sum.

Costs budgets in multi-track cases

Although consideration of the complexities of costs budgeting is beyond the scope of this book, the parties should familiarise themselves with the procedural requirements for costs budgets (CPR Part 3II) to be prepared whether for inclusion in the directions questionnaire where appropriate, and otherwise for the costs and case management conference listed after allocation to the multi-track. A failure to do so can prove devastating in terms of the financial implications on the client (or, more likely, their legal representative) as well as tactically when it comes to leverage for an advantageous settlement.

Part 36

The parties should never underestimate the power of an early Part 36 offer. Such offers can be made before the issue of proceedings: CPR r.36.7(1), and provide a useful incentive for the other side to engage meaningfully in mediation or ADR.

The value of Part 36 offers is self-evident and even more so where one or both parties are funding the litigation under the CFA regime.

POINTS TO NOTE

- **Where possible, follow the PD on pre-action conduct and protocols. Just because it cannot be done prior to issuing a claim or application for an injunction, does not mean it cannot be pursued thereafter. Keep concise but clear notes on what steps to comply were taken and when to assist on the question of costs if the time comes.**

- **Urgent injunctions should be sought where necessary for reinstatement or to prevent eviction.**

- **Unlawful eviction claims will be allocated to the Fast Track or the Multi Track, depending broadly on their value and complexity.**

- **Identify and collate your evidence early. If applications for delivery up of belongings (which may include bank statements, tenancy agreements etc.) are needed then they should be made urgently.**

- **Be prepared to make applications for unless orders or other sanctions in the event of any tactical delays during disclosure or any other part of the lead-up to trial.**

- Make sure costs budgets are filed and served on time where required.
- Do not forget the advantages of an early Part 36 offer, especially if acting for a landlord and the claimant is funded by a CFA.

MORE BOOKS BY LAW BRIEF PUBLISHING

A selection of our other titles available now:-

'Covid-19, Homeworking and the Law – The Essential Guide to Employment and GDPR Issues' by Forbes Solicitors
'Covid-19, Force Majeure and Frustration of Contracts – The Essential Guide' by Keith Markham
'Covid-19 and Criminal Law – The Essential Guide' by Ramya Nagesh
'Covid-19 and Family Law in England and Wales – The Essential Guide' by Safda Mahmood
'Covid-19 and the Implications for Planning Law – The Essential Guide' by Bob Mc Geady & Meyric Lewis
'Covid-19, Residential Property, Equity Release and Enfranchisement – The Essential Guide' by Paul Sams and Louise Uphill
'Covid-19, Brexit and the Law of Commercial Leases – The Essential Guide' by Mark Shelton
'Covid-19 and the Law Relating to Food in the UK and Republic of Ireland – The Essential Guide' by Ian Thomas
'A Practical Guide to the General Data Protection Regulation (GDPR) – 2nd Edition' by Keith Markham
'Ellis on Credit Hire – Sixth Edition' by Aidan Ellis & Tim Kevan
'A Practical Guide to Working with Litigants in Person and McKenzie Friends in Family Cases' by Stuart Barlow
'A Practical Guide to Secondary Liability and Joint Enterprise Post-Jogee' by Joanne Cecil & James Mehigan
'A Practical Guide to the Pre-Action RTA Claims Protocol for Personal Injury Lawyers' by Antonia Ford
'A Practical Guide to Neighbour Disputes and the Law' by Alexander Walsh

'A Practical Guide to Forfeiture of Leases' by Mark Shelton
'A Practical Guide to Coercive Control for Legal Practitioners and Victims' by Rachel Horman
'A Practical Guide to Rights Over Airspace and Subsoil' by Daniel Gatty
'Tackling Disclosure in the Criminal Courts – A Practitioner's Guide' by Narita Bahra QC & Don Ramble
'A Practical Guide to the Law of Driverless Cars – Second Edition' by Alex Glassbrook, Emma Northey & Scarlett Milligan
'A Practical Guide to TOLATA Claims' by Greg Williams
'Artificial Intelligence – The Practical Legal Issues' by John Buyers
'A Practical Guide to the Construction and Rectification of Wills and Trust Instruments' by Edward Hewitt
'A Practical Guide to the Law of Bullying and Harassment in the Workplace' by Philip Hyland
'How to Be a Freelance Solicitor: A Practical Guide to the SRA-Regulated Freelance Solicitor Model' by Paul Bennett
'A Practical Guide to Advising Clients at the Police Station' by Colin Stephen McKeown-Beaumont
'A Practical Guide to Antisocial Behaviour Injunctions' by Iain Wightwick
'Practical Mediation: A Guide for Mediators, Advocates, Advisers, Lawyers, and Students in Civil, Commercial, Business, Property, Workplace, and Employment Cases' by Jonathan Dingle with John Sephton
'The Mini-Pupillage Workbook' by David Boyle
'A Practical Guide to Spousal Maintenance' by Liz Cowell
'A Practical Guide to the Law of Domain Names and Cybersquatting' by Andrew Clemson
'A Practical Guide to the Law of Gender Pay Gap Reporting' by Harini Iyengar
'A Practical Guide to the Rights of Grandparents in Children Proceedings' by Stuart Barlow

'NHS Whistleblowing and the Law' by Joseph England
'Employment Law and the Gig Economy' by Nigel Mackay & Annie Powell
'A Practical Guide to Noise Induced Hearing Loss (NIHL) Claims' by Andrew Mckie, Ian Skeate, Gareth McAloon
'An Introduction to Beauty Negligence Claims – A Practical Guide for the Personal Injury Practitioner' by Greg Almond
'Zen and the Art of Mediation' by Martin Plowman
'A Practical Guide to the SRA Principles, Individual and Law Firm Codes of Conduct 2019 – What Every Law Firm Needs to Know' by Paul Bennett
'A Practical Guide to Adoption for Family Lawyers' by Graham Pegg
'A Practical Guide to Redundancy' by Philip Hyland
'A Practical Guide to Vicarious Liability' by Mariel Irvine
'A Practical Guide to Applications for Landlord's Consent and Variation of Leases' by Mark Shelton
'A Practical Guide to Relief from Sanctions Post-Mitchell and Denton' by Peter Causton
'A Practical Guide to Equity Release for Advisors' by Paul Sams
'A Practical Guide to the Law Relating to Food' by Ian Thomas
'A Practical Guide to Financial Services Claims' by Chris Hegarty
'The Law of Houses in Multiple Occupation: A Practical Guide to HMO Proceedings' by Julian Hunt
'A Practical Guide to Solicitor and Client Costs' by Robin Dunne
'Occupiers, Highways and Defective Premises Claims: A Practical Guide Post-Jackson – 2nd Edition' by Andrew Mckie
'A Practical Guide to Financial Ombudsman Service Claims' by Adam Temple & Robert Scrivenor
'A Practical Guide to Advising Schools on Employment Law' by Jonathan Holden

Printed in the USA
CPSIA information can be obtained
at www.ICGtesting.com
LVHW020842211023
761737LV00025B/609

9 781913 715236